I'M NOT OK, YOU'RE NOT OK, BUT THAT'S OK WITH GOD

Finding the Humor and Healing in Life

Shelley Hussey

With contributions by
James E. Mallory, M.D. and Melanie H. Wilson, Ph.D.

Published by
Harper Ink
www.harperink.biz

I'M NOT OK, YOU'RE NOT OK, BUT THAT'S OK WITH GOD
Finding the Humor and Healing in Life

For further information, contact the publisher: Harper Ink, www.harperink.biz.

The author has made every diligent effort to ensure that the information in this book is
accurate and complete. She assumes no responsibility for errors or omissions that are inad-
vertent or inaccurate, and makes no warranties or representations of any kind concerning the
safety of the information contained in this book. The information in this book is not
intended nor implied to be a substitute for professional medical advice. Please consult with
your doctor before using any information presented here for treatment. Nothing contained
in this book is intended to be for medical diagnosis or treatment. The views and opinions
expressed in the book are not intended to endorse any product or procedure.

ISBN: 978-0-615-19936-8

This book is dedicated to the memory
of my beautiful mom, Juanita Harper,
and to the vibrant life of Sheldon Harper,
the youngest octogenarian dad who ever was, and is.

Thanks for letting me swim in your gene pool.

Kudos for
I'm Not OK, You're Not OK, But That's OK With God

Some books make you feel guilty, some make you ashamed, others try and fix you with a heavy dose of "you-can-do-it," still others are so religious they put an anchor on the soul. Shelley Hussey has written a book that will set you free so you can dance before a God who loves "weird" people.

Steve Brown, Key Life Ministries, keylife.org

Here is a book as insightful, refreshing, and charming as the author herself. Shelley Hussey uses her intellectual humor in a way that makes readers reflect on their lives and rethink basic philosophies and coping mechanisms. This book is recommended reading for people dealing with illness, depression, or just the intricacies of everyday life.

Ricky Safer, President, PSC Partners Seeking a Cure, pscpartners.org

I'm Not OK is an engaging journey that will touch everyone at some level of a personalized 'semi-mental' trip. I particularly like the *Healing Words* and footnotes. The author provides technical insight in a delightful way that should give the ardent reader new 'handles of understanding.'

Paul L. Walker, Ph.D., Pastor, Author, International Speaker

What a wonderfully written book—the writing was as fun to read as the content. It's OK to not be OK, but it's not OK to not read this book!

Jennifer Schuchmann, Author, jenniferschuchmann.com, blog.jenniferschuchmann.com

The author has a funny, manic style and writes in "grit." I found myself laughing or crying along with her. She reminds us of the truth demonstrated by every crying baby or scared alcoholic or teenager who won't look under his bed after dark. There is little more powerful than a hug, a calm voice at 3 a.m., the strong hand of a loved one, or a conviction that someone or something watches over you and counts the feathers on your wings.

James Brody, Ph.D., Author, Evolutionary Psychology Forum Moderator, behavioronline.com

This book hits the nuttiness nail squarely on the head! Having a brother who suffers from many of the "cootie-type" idiosyncrasies addressed in *OK*, I can affirm the value of humor mingled with patience and understanding in maintaining some degree of personal sanity while fulfilling the caregiver role. The author's wit and keen insight helped me know that I am not alone in this struggle and that survival is a real possibility—a possibility that I often doubted.

Ron Furgerson, Pastor, New Life Christian Church, newlife4me.com

I highly recommend this delightful book! The author has identified and humorously written about psychological issues many baby boomers have experienced.

Richard H. Pfeiffer, Director, Growth Central, growthcentral.com

Contents

I'm Not OK, You're Not OK, But That's OK With God

Acknowledgements

- I acknowledge that the process of writing this book has been simultaneously a labor of love and lunacy.

- I acknowledge to the reader that this book is not perfect—because I'm not.

- I acknowledge the many who supported me along the way with their encouragement, artistic talent, and editing and proofing prowess:

My dad, my husband and children, Linda Kelly, Karen Maizel, Jennifer Schuchmann, Geni White, Phyllis DiMaria, Darla Givan, Ron Furgerson, Mariellen Jacobs, Carrie Brazil, Wanda Watson, Holly Kinney, Vicki West, Debbie Massa, Pam Inman, Nancy Fowler, Cathy Buchanan, Patricia Stuut, Celeste Dionne, Mary Eberhard, Jan Sixt, Victor Radinskiy, Alison White, Jim Greenwood for the fabulous cover (www.jimgreenwooddesign.com), Debbie Rohde for her endless patience and creative book layout (www.rohdemd.com), my writers' group members and mentors, and the *Shameless Husseys*.

- I acknowledge all those who allowed me to share their stories inside these pages. Your willingness to disclose your dysfunctions is admirable, even if some of you did wimp out and choose to remain anonymous.

- I acknowledge all the medical experts who contributed their knowledge to help us understand that most elusive and mysterious organ called the brain.

- A special acknowledgement to Melanie Wilson, Ph.D.—who, through some divine miracle, inspired and motivated me to complete this project. You are a *wonder.*

I thank God for all of you—and acknowledge Him too, for giving me the passion to write this message.

*Story is far older than the
art of science and psychology,
and will always be the elder in the equation
no matter how much time passes.*

Clarissa Pinkola Estes

Introduction

Definitions of bug: 1) a virus 2) a defect or imperfection 3) a craze or obsession

The Random House Dictionary[1]

For as long as I can remember, I have had bugs in my brain. My husband coined the phrase "bugs in my brain" after he noticed I was playing the piano . . . on my face. But I wasn't playing the piano; I was adding. I moved my fingers up and down my face like I was punching numbers on a calculator. But I can understand how my husband miscalculated what I was doing. Even I had a hard time describing my obsessive compulsions.

Other habits included scratching imaginary and real sores, nose twitching and picking, nail biting, and rubbing the ink off book pages with my knuckles. As a child, I loved reading so much that I absorbed every book I could get my hands on, literally. I rubbed my knuckles across the pages really fast. My knuckles burned from the friction of the fiction and turned gray from the rubbed-off ink. My favorite books were mysteries: the *Happy Hollisters, Trixie Belden,* and *Nancy Drew* series. Yet none were as mysterious as my knuckle nonsense.

Most kids do weird stuff—some chew their hair, scratch their fingers until they bleed, or maybe wear their underwear backward. Lots of us still do weird stuff, and maybe that's OK. But it's not OK when the weird stuff turns into depression, anxiety, or other emotional problems, causing confusion, embarrassment, and shame.

My purpose in writing this book: I believe that by employing a hybrid perspective of part memoir, part how-to, part self-help, and part laughter, I can help readers sort through some of their own issues. In the process I'll share stories from others' semi-mental journeys. By sharing these experiences I hope readers might be more inclined to talk with a friend, pastor, counselor, or doctor regarding their own stresses or long-term emotional problems.

Mental illness touches one out of four to five families,[2] and is no respecter of race, sex, financial status, or religion. Huge numbers of those affected suffer from the shame and blame that often coexist with their mental health challenges. My hope is that sufferers will come out of the closet and into the light, with a new understanding of their problems and new ways to deal with them. And even if you're not presently struggling with mental health issues yourself, maybe you'll gain empathy for the spouse, family member, or friend who is.

And because I'm not a psychiatrist or psychologist, I've asked those who are to give credibility to my mental meanderings. To that end, Dr. James Mallory, psychiatrist and retired director of the Atlanta Counseling Center, has contributed the footnotes and other "brain-speak" explanations in terms we can understand. Readers looking for practical advice on mental health topics discussed should see the *Mental Notes* at the back of the book, written by psychologist and author Dr. Melanie Wilson, whose comments are also interjected throughout these pages. A listing of several mental health resources follows *Mental Notes*.

If you're looking for a little inspiration and motivation, at the end of each chapter are applicable Scriptures and words of encouragement. Related note: I will often refer to Jesus as *Jay-sus*–it's a term of endearment.

Lastly, be advised that laughter is good medicine. If all anyone gleans from reading this book is a few laughs; well, I'll just be "tickled pink," as my mama used to say.

1

The Cooties

Half the world is nutty—the rest are squirrels.

Source Unknown

Be honest. You and I probably had some pretty strange childhood quirks. I know I did. Around my neighborhood in the '50s and '60s, the collective cultural name for these quirks was "the cooties." I'm not referring to lice or creepy-crawly bugs. Having the cooties was like being afflicted with emotional leprosy, or "bugs in the brain"—my husband's favorite term to describe nervous habits. Back then, kids avoided catching other kids' bugs or cooties by simultaneously yelling "Detours!" while holding up their thumbs.

It's possible I was born with the cooties, but they remained dormant until second grade, when I got glasses. My mom made the mistake of letting me pick out the frames for my spectacles, and I was a spectacle all right. The Coke-bottle-thick lenses sported fins that looked like they came from a pimp's '58 Cadillac. My self-esteem plummeted from the moment I put on my pimpin' glasses. Low self-esteem tended to set off an internal alarm, provoking nervous tics and twitches. I don't know why my glasses were such a big deal. Everybody on the planet who was nearsighted or farsighted wore "fins" at that time. Silly—how little things about our appearance affect us so early and so deeply.

In the early '60s, a twelve-year-old girl who wore anklets with dress shoes to school had cooties. Normal girls wore nylon stockings with dress shoes. And most twelve-year-olds slept in hair rollers with bobby pins stabbing their heads all night. Otherwise, they were losers. (Straight hair was of the devil in the '50s and '60s.) The slightest fashion faux pas could destroy one's self-esteem for the entire school year.

The Cooties

When I was eight or nine, I developed some slightly painful and disturbing habits, such as compulsively and fiercely scratching mosquito bites. I scratched with one hand, and typed on my face with the other. I also twitched my nose like a rabbit. I know the typing and twitching annoyed people because many twitched right back at me. I was be-twitched, bothered, and bewildered I was doing this stuff, but I couldn't stop. A)

The Pee-ano Lesson

One of my most embarrassing childhood moments happened because I was extremely shy. During a piano lesson when I was eleven, I tinkled on the piano bench. I was too bashful to ask to use the bathroom, even though my bladder was ready to burst. By the end of the lesson, I had soaked the bench. My teacher didn't notice the puddle, but she did notice that I suddenly shifted from the key of F-minor. I was in Pee-major. When the lesson finally ended, I backed out of the room and then out of the house so the teacher wouldn't notice my wet backside.

Splish-Splash, I'm Not Taking a Bath

As a child, I wanted nothing to do with puberty. Puberty was the launching pad to adulthood, and I *never* wanted to be an adult. From what I observed, adulthood was too much responsibility and not enough fun.

With my own weird thought processes operating, I thought I could stop myself from growing up if I quit wearing deodorant. I also quit taking a bath for several months, and I am not making this up. I ran the bath water and made splish-splash sounds to fool my parents, but unfortu-nately I frequently forgot to splish-splash the towel. My parents, known for their cleverness, eventually uncovered my dirty little secret and forced me to clean up my act.

A) Nervous habits are part of the spectrum of obsessive-compulsive disorders. The individual usually has nervous tension, which becomes a conditioned reflex and is difficult to interrupt.

Section Eight

My shyness and nervous habits followed me to junior high school—that time of life when everyone gets weird. I continued to wear the glasses with the Cadillac fins, now the upgraded '61 model with all the options. Back then, our local school administrators didn't concern themselves with children's self-esteem issues. They organized kids in sections, ranging from Section One for smart kids to Section Nine for Special Ed. I was in Section Eight, dangerously close to special-ness. (My dad says that "Section Eight" was a qualification for a mental discharge from the military.) On the first day of school, everyone asked everyone else, "What section are you in?" Whenever I was asked, I lied. I told them, "Section Seven," which to me sounded a whole lot smarter than "Section Eight."

A Shell of My Former Self

As puberty continued to engulf me, life became more painful, so I decided that twelve would be my age limit. By fourteen I realized my plan wasn't working. I needed to take drastic measures to stop the age progression, so I decided to try the starvation diet, otherwise known as anorexia nervosa. B)

Eating disorders were not popular in the '60s. The popular diseases of the time were strep throat, tonsillitis, and mono—same as now minus the currently rampant eating and other psychological disorders. Most of my classmates thought I had mono, but I never corrected them, mainly because I didn't know what to tell them. I was satisfied with my emaciated appearance, and for the first time in awhile, I felt in control of one area of my life: my food intake.

I was also lacking in mental clarity. I thought seventy-eight pounds looked good on my 5'4" frame. Our family doctor wasn't impressed however, and she recommended I see a psychologist.

B) Anorexia is a form of addiction. Like all addictions, anorexia nervosa centers on a focal point: in this case, not eating or drinking. Anorexics have an incredible ability to deny their problem, and are best treated in a group setting

---

The next day after I arrived home from school, I noticed a manicure gift set on my bed. *Uh-oh,* I said to myself, having that instinctively uneasy feeling that dogs must get when they know they're going to the vet. The gift was my mom's way of smoothing over my initial visit to the psychologist.

Sitting stiffly in the psychologist's office wearing my red winter coat with the real fur collar, I waited apprehensively for him to speak. When he finally did, he lost me with his psychobabbling. I never went back to see him, but I did go see the Beatles.

I was so obsessed with the Beatles that I begged my parents to drive me 300 miles to Chicago to see them perform. They succumbed, thinking the trip might be a form of shock therapy. Unfortunately, the Beatles trip did nothing to change my ingrained, diseased thought patterns. I didn't snap out of my anorectic stupor until a few months later, when my parents threatened to put me in the hospital. I was one of the lucky ones. About half of all girls suffering from anorexia nervosa never recover.[1]

There was only one other case of anorexia in my high school that I was aware of: a girl who was 5'6", fifty-some pounds, and valedictorian of the senior class. Eventually she became rather heavy. Her weight bounced around quite a bit, and she died by the age of twenty-five. I never learned the cause of her death, but I've always wondered if her extreme weight fluctuation was a major contributor.

I didn't discover that my own problem was a disorder until the mid-'70s, when I read an article about anorexia nervosa in a Sunday news-magazine. I was stunned to find out there was a name for this "thing" I had as a teen. The article said that anorexia was more than a passing fad among teenage girls, but I don't recall any concrete reasons listed as to the cause.

Bug Charisma

After recovering from anorexia, I continued to have awful eating habits, especially once I moved out of my parents' house. My diet mainstay was sugary cereal or donuts in the morning, cookies and candy in the afternoon, and brownies, cakes, or pies at suppertime. I felt jumpy, edgy, irritable, unfocused, restless, and had heart palpitations. My addiction to sugar was so strong that I woke up several times in the middle of the night for years, and went into the kitchen to eat something sweet. C) In my desperation to stop the nocturnal kitchen raids, I visited a hypnotist, who failed to entrance me. My next solution was to have my apartment roommate lock me into my bedroom at night. The locked door strategy worked for only a week because my roommate had her own mental health issues. She was evicted for attacking her mother, who lived in our same apartment complex.

Apparently I had "bug charisma"—an innate ability to connect with highly unstable people. Or perhaps being around such people raised my self-esteem. Or maybe my bugs attracted theirs, kind of like a porch light in the summer.

Years later I learned about the psychological and biochemical components of food addiction. People use food for immediate gratification, to relieve depression, stress, or boredom, or to rebel.[2] Eating disorders can coexist with anxiety, kleptomania, repetitive self-mutilation, depression, alcoholism, or personality disorders.[3]

Like most food addicts, I was attempting to self-medicate through a massive ingestion of carbohydrates. Carbohydrates increase the level of a calming brain chemical called serotonin.[4] Apparently, I was born a quart low in serotonin, gauging from the dipstick of my early life.

My parents tried to be supportive, but they were mostly puzzled about all my nervous habits and eating disorder. Connecting with me was very difficult.

Our Family: The Slightly Dysfunctional Cleavers

My mom was the perfect June Cleaver type. She was flawlessly groomed at all times—although she and June parted company when it came to wearing pearls and shirtwaist dresses. My mother's life was wrapped up in doing typical '50s and '60s stuff for our family. Sometimes Mom worked herself into such a frazzle with cooking, cleaning, washing, ironing, and yelling at us four kids that she came to the dinner table

---

C) Diets deficient in basic vitamins, minerals, or calories make a person more vulnerable to whatever mental condition they're genetically predisposed toward. A severe vitamin B deficiency can cause mental illness, for instance, though it is rare in this country.

exhausted, laying her head down on the table while the rest of us ate.

Dad used to warn us, "You kids need to behave or Mom is going to have a nervous breakdown." I later learned that monthly migraines contributed to Mom's frazzled state. An imbalance of hormones combined with severe pain is enough to make any woman go tilt.

I was very sensitive to her mood swings. If she was acting stressed, I'd feel jittery. If I saw her lying in her recliner all day, I knew she was either depressed and/or stressed.

Mom gained a significant amount of weight in her forties. My instincts told me that her weight gain was connected to her mental state, but we didn't discuss the matter. Discussing depression in the '60s and '70s just wasn't . . . discussed. The only depression my mom understood was the one she suffered through in the '30s. But Mom finally got happy after her major stressors left: us kids.

My dad was the typical father of that era, except he was a lot more fun than Ward Cleaver. When he came home from work, he always found time and energy to play "I'm Gonna Get Ya!" Dad chased us through the house while we screamed and ran to the closet. His great imagination fabricated games like "Make a Slaff" ("Make Us Laugh"). He'd line us up and make faces or weird noises until everyone laughed—and I was usually the last laugher.

I certainly couldn't blame my parents for my problems, except possibly in a genetic sense. My family would not have been classified as dysfunctional in the cultural framework of that time period. However, I recently heard a counselor on the radio give a great definition of a dysfunctional home: "A home where you don't feel free to trust, feel, or talk." If that is an accurate definition, then every family I knew was dysfunctional, including mine. The biggest trauma I faced at home was having my older brother call me "Shelley Belly," which was pretty mild compared to my modern-day moniker: "Shameless Hussey."

Our family did normal things: ate meals together, played board games, watched Ed Sullivan, lived in a middle-class neighborhood, took vacations in our Rambler station wagon, and owned a neurotic beagle who had dog cooties. We were a slice of midwestern and mid-twentieth century Americana—befitting of a Norman Rockwell painting.

In retrospect, it's obvious that my mom was suffering from bouts of anxiety and depression, and of course I swam in that gene pool. Additionally, my paternal grandmother was hit with a blast of anxiety genes, which skipped my dad, worked their way into my brain, and implanted bugs. D) In turn, I passed along my bug collection to my kids.

Bugging My Kids

My son James had a most peculiar habit of stretching out his socks about eight inches at the toes. He then folded his socks over his feet before putting on his shoes. He claimed the folded-over socks made his shoes more comfortable. It bugged me when he did that, so I persuaded him to stop with a $20 bribe. Now, as an adult male, his sock habits are perfectly normal. He takes them off and throws them in the middle of the floor.

James was also extremely shy as a child. Extremely. One night a pastor and his wife came to visit. We asked James, then age three, to come and meet the company. James introduced himself by crawling into the living room on all fours, head tucked under as if he was vacuuming the carpet. Once James made his entrance, there was a vacuum in the conversation as well. Fred and I tried to get James to stand up and say hello, but he refused to stand *or* speak. We were all embarrassed, not knowing what to say about our son's strange behavior. The pastor and his wife graciously looked the other way and talked quietly between themselves while Fred and I did our best impression of the "Jaws of Life" to dislodge James from the carpet.

Both my son and daughter were painfully shy as children. They may have been exhibiting selective mutism, a disorder characterized by consistent failure to speak in certain social settings.[5] Until my kids started kindergarten, they spoke to no one over four feet tall, except close relatives, other kids, and really short friends of mine.

Thankfully, James is not quite as shy at twenty-nine; his quirks have matured along with him. He, like his dad, paces and scratches his head, often at the same time. And according to reports from his roommate, he no longer vacuums the carpet with his head, or any other body part.

My daughter also had a few compulsive tendencies. On Mary Beth's fourth birthday, we gave her a Rainbow Brite doll and My Little Pony: two popular toys of the mid-'80s. Mary Beth took the doll and pony show

---

D) It is now believed that all mental disorders have a genetic component. In fact there are probably multiple genes involved. If one has enough multiple genes, the predisposition to having a mental illness is increased.

---

everywhere for six months. If we left the house without one or both toys, she had a preschool version of a panic attack. Finally we heard from God concerning this behavior. Her Sunday school teacher insisted that Mary Beth leave both toys at home if she wanted to come to Sunday school, and that settled it. Mary Beth abandoned her idols, replacing them with crackers, juice, and Jesus.

Mary Beth's latest thing as a young adult is to faint at the doctor's office after she has her blood drawn. She convinces herself she's dehydrated from the itty-bitty blood loss. As Gilda Radner's quirky character Roseanna Roseanna Dana used to say: "There is always something!"

Salvation Through Bladder Polyps

I had little awareness of God throughout my youth. He and I were formally introduced when I was twenty-five years old.

For several months I attended a youth ministry called "Gospel House Rap" with my boyfriend, a born-again Christian. I didn't plan to answer the altar call to "get saved." I was divinely tricked. I misunderstood— probably due to having fallen asleep. I thought I heard the pastor say, "If anyone in your family needs prayer for healing, please come forward." So, with some manipulative nudging from my boyfriend, I went to the altar to save Grandpa from his precancerous bladder polyps. But darned if I didn't end up getting saved instead.

Five minutes later, those of us at the altar were led to the "recovery room" as I call it, where a sensitive counselor explained the gospel in a nutshell: ". . . if you confess with your mouth, 'Jesus is Lord,' and believe in your heart that God raised him from the dead, you will be saved" (Romans 10:9).

My life changed overnight. I began to experience moments of peace. I still had bugs in my brain, but God had debugged my heart. *Praise Jay-sus.*

Healing Words

Philippians 4:7 says: "And the peace of God, which transcends all understanding, will guard your hearts and your minds in Christ Jesus."

The world may give us riches, friends, and more, but it cannot give us peace. Peace comes from God alone. When our minds are troubled, God understands and wants to comfort us and help us rise above our circumstances. God loves us unconditionally, cooties and all.

"A cheerful heart is good medicine, but a crushed spirit dries up the bones." Proverbs 17:22

One of the greatest gifts God has given us is a sense of humor. But we can't enjoy it if we take ourselves too seriously. Laughter enriches relationships, overrides painful circumstances, and is good for the soul.

I'M NOT OK

2

From Band-Aid Soup to Nuts

The statistics on sanity are that one out of every four Americans is suffering from some form of mental illness. Think of your three best friends. If they're okay, then it's you.

Rita Mae Brown

So here I am on the second leg of life, having graduated from childhood quirks to more mature types of nervous or emotional problems. I notice roadblocks that result in detours on the path to a tranquil mind. However, holding up my thumbs and yelling "Detours!" no longer immunizes me from catching cooties. Besides, I've been a carrier since childhood.

Good Golly, It's Folly!

My newfound faith encouraged me. But I was conflicted and convicted about my sugar addiction. Sweets were still ruling my mind even though Jay-sus—as I fondly refer to him—was inside my heart.

I once asked a group of women to pray for my deliverance from the sugar demon, and eventually I was sugar-freed, through prayer, determination, and education. Proverbs 15:14 says, "The discerning heart seeks knowledge, but the mouth of a fool feeds on folly." Webster's Dictionary[1] defines folly as: "Lack of good judgment, an instance of foolishness, an excessively costly and often unprofitable undertaking." Regarding the "excessively costly" part—my sugar addiction was expensive. Over the years I spent thousands of dollars on dental fillings and crowns due to my sweet teeth. Such folly—to feed my face this way.

Shortly after I wed husband Fred, I bought a book called *Sugar Blues* by William Dufty (Warner Books). The book's arguments against sugar were so compelling that I decided to give it up cold turkey. With a lot of support from Fred—*"Get your butt back in bed!"*—I quit my night time visits to the refrigerator. After I eliminated the sugar in my diet, I calmed down. But I still had a somewhat wired outlook on life.

Band-Aid Soup

When I attained a little peace of mind and made mental headway in one area of my life, another roadblock popped up. Immediately after claiming victory over my nocturnal eating habits, I started waking up several times at night again. This time *I* wasn't eating—someone else was.

For several years I was sleep-deprived. I finally figured out the problem: babies. Babies were my catalyst for walking the path to perfectionist perdition. I sewed, nursed my kids until they were nine years old—it felt like—although it was probably closer to nineteen *months,* and made all meals, including homemade bread, from scratch. Now that I'm older and wiser, I rarely allow myself to become sleep-deprived *or* pregnant.

Sleep deprivation coupled with domestic perfectionism took their toll. I became more irritable, developed bigger bugs in my brain, and baked Band-Aids in my soup.

"Band-Aid Soup" was a recipe I concocted after one sleepless night. It takes no special skill to make Band-Aid Soup. However, it tastes best if the cook is exhausted when putting the ingredients together. Here's my secret recipe:

Wake up tired, then chop a bunch of vegetables and throw them in a pot. Chop a clove of garlic carelessly so that you cut your finger. Now put a Band-Aid on your finger. The Band-Aid eventually slips off your finger and falls in the soup. When you serve the soup, your husband will get the bowl containing the Band-Aid. He will be upset when he chews it. To avoid future confrontation, simply switch bowls with your husband so that you eat the Band-Aid.

Unnatural Childbirth

Moms who gave birth in the '70s and '80s made a big deal about natural childbirth. We natural mothers used to gloat: "I had natural childbirth—did you?" *But what's natural about a thirty-five-and-a-half-hour labor?* I've heard women say they don't remember the pain of childbirth because they're so overjoyed at having a baby. I say their brains got pushed out with their placentas. My son was almost an only child; that's how overjoyed I was.

Blissfully unaware of the perils of the impending delivery, and maternal maverick of the '70s that I was, I gave birth to James in a double bed in one of the country's first home-like birthing centers. A nurse-midwife handled the long and arduous delivery, and the doctor circumcised the baby right in our room. It was horrible, and I decided if I ever had another baby, she would be a girl.

I went home in twenty-four hours so I could bond with the baby. Little did I know that instead of bonding I'd feel like bouncing the baby on his little head.

During the ride home from the hospital, I felt like throwing James out the car window. I didn't *want* to throw James out the window; I just thought I *might.*

I've since found out that other friends had thoughts of throwing their babies out the window too. None of them wanted to; they just thought they might. They, like me, were exhausted and stressed, with some suffering from postpartum depression. A)

Fortunately, I became aware of a potent protein powder that perked me up toward the end of the period I call my Band-Aid Soup Daze. I began drinking the protein after a friend said, "You look terrible. You need to try this protein powder." Thirty minutes after a dose I felt a surge of energy and my outlook became more positive.

A) Postpartum depression has often been untreated because it is assumed that the mother simply has the post-baby blues, a problem that normally clears up on its own. However, if she has the cardinal symptoms of depression: sleep disorders, loss of interest in normal activities, guilt, decreased energy, trouble concentrating, being slowed down mentally or physically, and thoughts of suicide with symptoms lasting longer than two weeks, she needs professional treatment.

Emotional Blind Spots

When I didn't have the energy or courage to deal with problems, I tended to overlook them. I called those unresolved issues "emotional blind spots."

For instance, my son was born with a minor birth defect called congenital torticollis, or wryneck syndrome. The problem showed up when he was two weeks old. I saw a huge lump on the side of his neck and feared the worst: cancer. I didn't have the energy or courage to confront that possibility, so I ignored the lump. Thank God my husband noticed, or the kid might have grown up with his head permanently bent over his left shoulder. After a doctor's visit and X-rays, we began therapy. James' neck and head straightened out when he was four months old, due to physical therapy—and prayer—I'm convinced. *(Praise Jay-sus.)*

The closer I got to a painful truth, the more I seemed to fear it. Reality became too difficult to deal with. Scared, I ended up in denial, perpetuating the pattern of refusing to meet things head-on. These factors contributed to my mental or emotional blind spots.

"Zucchini-Land"

My puzzled husband* was emotionally blind to my angst during those early years of our marriage. He honestly did not know what my problem was. We had an adequate bank account, a healthy baby, and no major outside stresses. Fred's cute nickname for me during those early, blurry years was "zucchini," because of my constant vegetative state.

Since vegetables need to grow, and I was a young, green Christian, I went to a weekly Bible study. One night I brought the baby along. The pastor who led the study looked at James and said to me, "You know, this is the easiest time to be a parent, so enjoy it. Things will get much harder. Just wait till the teenage years." I am happy to report that his prophecy was unfulfilled. Teenagers sleep a lot, unlike babies.

---

*As I share my story over the next several chapters, it may seem as if I make Fred look like a jerk. That's because back then he was, but so was I. We still are jerks, but we love each other anyway.

When I was sleep-deprived, B) my thinking was distorted. I was forgetful, irritable, anxious, depressed, and had panic episodes. My insomniac routine went like this: Wake up after a few hours of sleep, heart starts palpitating, feel bogeyman's clutches, look up sleep Scriptures and try to meditate on them.

British writer Aldous Huxley said, "That we are not much sicker and much madder than we are is due exclusively to that most blessed and blessing of all natural graces, sleep." Amen, Brother Aldous.

When Life Gets Tough, Get Donuts

When James was seven months old, I gave up health foods and vitamins. I had high expectations that my good diet would solve all my problems, and it failed me. I fell back on my comfort food. Whenever life got tough, I got donuts.

Every morning for several months, I put baby James in the stroller and walked the half-mile to the corner donut shop, rationalizing that the walking would eradicate any donut damage. I always picked out the same donuts: two chocolate-covered long johns with whipped cream filling. The donuts were temporarily satisfying, but they still left a hole.

For some time, I've been a recovering Donut Diva, limiting myself to an occasional Krispy Kreme—still the chocolate-covered, whipped cream filling confection. It's all about balance and moderation. I balance the occasional donut in one hand and the moderately-hot coffee in the other.

Poop for Brains

During my life I've made a few bad decisions. One poor choice was to take our toddler son and accompany my husband on a month-long

---

B) Sleep deprivation studies have been done on depressed people. If they are prevented from sleeping over a twenty-four-hour period, there is temporary improvement of depression. However, in general, people who are chronically sleep-deprived become far more vulnerable to whatever they are genetically predisposed toward. Virtually 100 percent of all people will have hallucinations if they are deprived of sleep long enough.

---

business trip. The trip ended up being a giant poop sandwich, partly because baby James had a bad case of diarrhea, but also due to my sick-and-tired, never-fully-recovered-from-childbirth-state. I was still nursing James and had developed a double breast infection. My fever and exhaustion produced unnerving thoughts.

I was walking the baby in his stroller by an embankment one day, and I thought I might throw him down the hill. I didn't *want* to, I just thought I *might*. Déjà vu from bringing him home in the car as a newborn.

On December 12, 1980, at sixteen months of age, James started sleeping through the night. That night our second child was conceived. Maternal instinct, combined with short-term memory loss, won over the voice of reason. I probably should have spaced my pregnancies better, but since I was so spaced out, my common sense flew out the window.

Wake Up! It's Not the Coffee!

One of my resources for spiritual support during this time was a Christian women's luncheon where, five months pregnant and suffering from nervous exhaustion, I went forward for prayer. The going-forward took great courage on my pregnant part, because the Pentecostal preacher could easily have been one of those "shove her in the forehead and knock her out till she's healed!" kind of guys. However, I must have caught him on a day when he was feeling more Presbyterian than Pentecostal. He simply laid a hand on my shoulder, looked deeply into my bloodshot, exhausted eyes, and said three words: "Cut out caffeine."

The amount of coffee I was drinking wouldn't have roused a napping gnat. Caffeine was not the cause of my problem, but I sure wanted to believe the preacher dude's words.

The Burning Bug

Things were semi-OK until I did another dumb thing. I took a trip with Fred and our two kids: a two-year-old and a newborn. Our five-hour drive to Cincinnati was uneventful except for our car catching on fire. And there I go with that obsessive thought about throwing the baby out the window, but at least this time it was to save my baby's life, not because my brain was fried. Our VW Bug was fried, however, and burned to the ground. We jumped out of the car, grabbing nothing but the kids. But we did salvage a few things: a parched $20 bill and two pairs of hickory-smoked underwear.

Around the time of the Burning Bug episode, my two-week-old daughter commenced screaming for hours every night. The colic medication didn't work, but fortunately her gas pains stopped after a few months. I was ready to throw myself out the window at that point. It wouldn't have done any good; we lived in a one-story house.

My kids are now grown and gone and, believe me, dealing with adult children's issues is a delight compared to enduring sleepless nights with babies. If given a choice, I would have preferred giving birth to *adult* children. Tough labors don't scare me—been there, done that.

Any vestiges of my "Amish Martha Stewart" days of bread baking and cooking from scratch are long gone, and the biblical Martha in me is fatally wounded, too. (Martha was always cooking, cleaning, and complaining.) Fred is now the Martha in our family. But he doesn't clean. He just cooks and complains. That's OK. I'm happy with two out of three.

Tripping Out on Tryptophan

In the late '80s and early '90s, tryptophan, an amino acid touted as a natural tranquilizer,[2] was quite popular. Unfortunately, a bad batch was manufactured in Japan, killing a few people, so the FDA removed it from US store shelves. For a couple of years while tryptophan was on the market, I used it to slow myself down from a record 78 rpm to 33 1/3, as we used to say in pre-CD days.

I must have been so tripped out on trytophan that I thought having baby number three was a good idea. Unfortunately, Fred was not tripping out with me, and he did not like the idea. I had always wanted a third child, even though my brain was telling me in all caps: NO MORE BABIES! My competitive nature and my maternal instincts overruled my rational thought processes.

Since Fred was against baby number three, knowing my limits better than I did, I had to form a pregnancy coup and take over his body. Before Fred knew what had happened, I was pregnant. When I was eighteen weeks along, an ultrasound showed the baby had died. No cause was ever found for the baby's death.

My emotions were quite jumbled about losing the baby. I was upset yet relieved, grieving yet peaceful. Apparently God knew better than I did what I could and couldn't handle.

Sisters-in-Law Should Be Outlawed

A huge chunk of my self-worth was based upon my performance as a family member. And I was performing fairly well until my brothers and brother-in-law selfishly took brides for themselves.

I simply could not compete with the culinary skills of my three energetic, ethnic background, cooking-in-their-blood sisters-in-law. One was Russian, one was Hungarian, one was Greek, and I was the Geek. Those three could bedazzle you with their hospitality and entertaining; meanwhile I'm offering up Band-Aid Soup. (See recipe on page 22.)

The good news: I no longer think of myself as a family competitor, mainly because I've given up. Instead, I think of myself as "unique," which is what everyone else thinks they are, so I'm in good company.

Healing Words

"We have this hope as an anchor for the soul, firm and secure." Hebrews 6:19

When our world is crashing in around us, we can put our hope in God. Just as an anchor holds a ship safely in position, our hope in God guarantees our ultimate safety, in spite of our circumstances. Never give up hope.

"The wise in heart are called discerning, and pleasant words promote instruction." Proverbs 16:21

Johann Wolfgang von Goethe said, "Correction does much, but encouragement does more." When we're feeling weak and vulnerable, we want to be enveloped in compassion and caring, yet we sometimes feel only judgment and condemnation. As you go through anxiety or depression, choose your friends and advisors wisely.

Rural Georgia, January 1990

Country Cookin'

Donna Brooks

Worst Cooking Fiascos

I was extremely tired one night and was trying to make vegetable soup. While I was chopping garlic, I cut my finger, so I put a Band-aid on it. As I was dropping the vegetables into the soup, my wet Band-aid slipped in, unannounced. We sat down to eat, and as my husband bit into the Band-aid, he freaked out! A week later, still tired, I made another batch of soup, and the whole scenario was repeated. Again, my husband flipped out! So to save our marriage, whenever I'm tired and make soup, I just switch bowls with my husband.

Shelley Hussey
Acworth

3

The Fleeting Peace of Mind Zip Code

God loves you just the way you are, but He loves you too much to let you stay like this.

As seen on a bumper sticker

The cruise ship hypnotist began the show in his soothing, monotone voice: "Relax and close your eyes. Empty your mind of distractions. Think of a place that's calm, peaceful, and serene . . . perhaps a warm, tropical climate with clean, sandy beaches and vast blue skies, where no one hurries, and life is simple and tranquil. You're safe there. Now go to that happy place and think happy thoughts."

Immediately I was transported back to the happy place of South Carolina in the mid-'80s, where I thought lots of happy thoughts. Columbia, South Carolina, was an on-and-off, three-year rest stop for my mind. Yet curiously, I still overreacted to little stresses. But I tried not to dwell on these reactions since I wanted to believe I was no longer fragile.

For the most part, life in Columbia was like the movie *Groundhog Day,* about a guy (Bill Murray) who relives the same day over and over. We woke up every morning in a tropical-like environment, complete with palm trees. Our frequent visits to the neighborhood pool made life feel like a constant vacation. The downside: I was depressed due to losing the baby and the fact that I couldn't make friends. I had always depended on friends to meet my emotional needs, and I thought the South was known for its hospitality. *"How y'all doin'? Would y'all like some swayte* (sweet) *tay* (tea)?" You know, that kind of thing. I wasn't counting on culture shock. I thought Americans were the same, except for the drawl, whether living north or south of the Mason-Dixon Line. They're not.

Dixie Chicks

I was a no-nonsense, fast-talkin,' nasal-twangin' Yankee girl, wearing whatever Salvation Army had on sale that week, and these South Carolina chicks were slow-talkin,' Dixie-drawlin' Southern belles with in vogue clothes, perfect hair, make-up, and nails. They didn't get me and I didn't get them. But we were all ever-so polite and pretended everything was fine.

The South Carolina church chicks weren't crazy about me either, but to their credit, they did ask me to be their Bible study teacher. The first study I taught was on attaining peace of mind. A "piece of my mind" is what I really wanted to give them.

The Elusive Peace of Mind Zip Code

I felt pretty confident about teaching the Peace of Mind study—my brain bugs were lying dormant at the time. I told my Southern sisters to get rid of pride, envy, and lust if they wanted to find peace. Pray, be humble, enjoy fellowship, control your thought processes. Piece of cake, this peace of mind stuff.

But I wasn't being real. I never let anyone know that for most of my life I had been buggy, or that everyday stresses were daunting, and that during those times the peace of mind zip code eluded me. To admit I had a problem might have diminished my reputation, and I was trying to gain acceptance among these Dixie chicks. I wanted everyone to think I could follow my own advice.

Any stress reactions that did surface I attributed to weak faith or a character flaw. I knew nothing about the brain's powerful biochemistry and its ability to temporarily hijack my peace of mind. It never occurred to me there might be a biological reason for an anxiety flare-up. If anyone knew about the biochemical roots of depression or anxiety in the early to mid-'80s, they weren't broadcasting it on my TV or radio.

The thing that would throw me into a near-terminal tizzy quicker than anything else during the Dixie Chick Days was overnight guests. I turned on my performance-mode switch, which turned on the anxiety-mode switch. *How and what was I going to cook? What would people think if they noticed my windows were dirty?*

An astonishing revelation came to me: No one honestly cares about my/your windows. When people come to visit, they're coming to see us, not our windows. When they want to see windows, they go to Home Depot. Too bad I didn't know that then. The only people who could visit me and not trigger a tizzy were my parents. I sensed unconditional love from them.

I Meet My Clone—It's In the Cards

In the movie *It's a Wonderful Life,* Clarence gives George Bailey the book *Tom Sawyer,* with this inscription: "Dear George, remember no man is a failure who has friends."

While men's friendships revolve around activities, women's friendships develop around sharing.[1] Yet, because of the culture shock in South Carolina, I had trouble knowing how to share or connect . . . until Linda came along.

Linda was totally nuts, in a good way. She was also from Texas, but I don't think that means anything; I know normal people from Texas. She was spontaneous, like me. The first time I met her I asked her to be an equal partner in a business, and she agreed.

We used our talents to create huge portrait cards, which we delivered in person, complete with song parodies and goofy adlibs. My—and Linda's—self-esteem shot up about five notches during our eighteen months in business. The increased self-esteem was great, but our constant cutting up and laughter was even better. Perhaps the laughter kept the bugs in my brain from bugging me.

Laughing and Leaking

Studies show that laughter not only promotes a feeling of wellbeing, but also relaxes and unwinds your stress knots, lowers your blood pressure, strengthens your immune system, and improves your circulation.[2] Scientists have found that children laugh an average of 400 times a day, while we crabbier adults laugh an average of only fifteen times a day.[3]

Laughter also tends to provoke a loss of bladder control when you're an adult, but Linda and I didn't care. We occasionally leaked and frequently laughed while delivering our super-sized singing greeting cards. (Of note: The leaks came back fifteen years later, and now it's *not* funny.)

The Audacity of Change

My three-year-long, mostly stress-free vacation ended. Fred got transferred to Atlanta. I did not want to move to that high-stressed, fast-paced, traffic-jamming zip code. I preferred the peace of mind zip code.

Besides my friendship with Linda, I eventually developed close relationships with several other women—Dixie chicks included. My initial culture shock had given way to culture comfort. Leaving behind close friends and a growing business that I loved was an uncomfortable proposition.

With the business growth came stress, but not enough to overwhelm me or make me dysfunctional. I had mini-anxiety attacks, that's all. I regretfully sold my half of the business.

One part of me was relieved to be moving on. When my friends had problems, I often spent my energy helping them and sometimes felt drained. My psychiatric nurse friend Geni White calls this "rescuer syndrome." Since I didn't know how to deal effectively with the problem of allowing people to overwhelm me, moving was an escape.

City Dixie Chicks Retreat

The Dixie chicks in Atlanta were not at all like the Dixie chicks in South Carolina. I determined this must be a cultural aberration. The women all had casually styled hair, wore minimal make-up, and bought their clothes at Target or consignment stores. Immediately accepted, I felt great. Atlanta is a very cosmopolitan city and the people liked my outrageous personality and self-deprecating humor. Here the churchy Dixie chicks wanted to be my friends, but they did *not* want me to teach their Bible studies. They did, however, want me to be a part of their yearly retreat. I was such a "crazy" person, wouldn't I be a lot of fun?

A spiritual retreat is a splendid idea, especially for those who stress out easily and need a breather for the brain and spirit. Merriam-Webster's Dictionary[4] defines retreat as: "a period of group withdrawal for prayer, meditation, study, and instruction under a director." However, I've observed that some well-meaning and hardworking retreat organizers are too busy planning their events to focus on basic comfort needs of the attendees. I was a retreat planner once (key word: *once*), so what I'm about to say makes me guilty too.

From my experience, a retreat consists of a bunch of stressed out women who:

- spend a sleepless night in a crowded room on uncomfortable beds,

- have schedules filled to the brim with so much stuff they're forced to go to bed late and get up early,

- dine on fattening, sugar-laden, constipating food, and

- try to learn more stuff the next morning, but are too tired and bloated to concentrate.

The morning speaker—who feels great because she took a laxative and had a full night's sleep on a firm mattress in her private room—sees that everyone's nodding off. She has the ladies stretch a few minutes to shake the cobwebs from their brains. It doesn't work. It's possible they'll grasp an enlightening truth or two and enjoy a few laughs, but they'll be so tired, the memories from the weekend will blur.

I went on the above-described retreat. Spending the night was not part of my plan, so I didn't bother bringing an overnight bag. The arrangement was for me to attend the evening program with another woman, who would then drive us both home. However, treacherous, stormy weather ensued and I was stuck at the mountain retreat. I had no sleeping bag, pajamas, deodorant, or toothbrush. It was like being on *Survivor,* only I *wanted* to be the first one kicked off the mountain.

My sense of foreboding and panic led to insomnia, heart palpitations, and racing, negative thoughts that lasted all night. The aftereffects would continue for days. One night's loss of sleep could spin my fragile brain out of control. My mind would wind up tighter than a top, then unwind slowly. I learned a valuable lesson: Do a quick retreat whenever anyone mentions retreat.

Flight Club

Racing, negative thoughts and heart palpitations are possible even without a trigger such as sleeplessness. Sometimes I would have no idea what triggered the fearful feelings that exploded in my mind's minefield. Regardless, my brain perceived enough stressful "hits" to upset the delicate chemistry, causing my pre-wired fight-or-flight response. A)

Not being a violent person, my brain prefers flight to fight. I can now pinpoint and often prevent the triggers that cause my flight responses. Recognizing the warning signs gives me some control over my anxiety.

I'm also able to delay my flights through aerobic walking and tennis. Just about everyone knows that exercise improves both physical and mental health, decreases stress levels, and encourages calmness. In some instances, exercise can reverse anxiety and depression.[5]

In the late '80s I started an exercise program. But thirty minutes of walking a day was not enough. My anxiety episodes overran each other and increased in intensity. My brain kept taking off, but never landed. I collected thousands of frequent flight-er miles. The flights began departing more frequently. And I couldn't identify any outside triggers that started the engines. My babies were now preteens—that perfect age when you don't worry about them at night—halfway between crying fits and driver's licenses. However, intrusive, free-floating, irrational negative thoughts and fears kept me awake and later consumed me. The thought I most obsessed over was: *What will people think of me if I can't live up to their expectations regarding blah, blah?*

As long as everything was peaceful and quiet, I could stay grounded and maintain minimal function. But if anybody offended me, or showed disapproval in any way, or asked me to make a decision, I was no longer able to cool my jets. As a member of the Flight Club, my brain would be cleared for take off. It was one bumpy ride.

A) The brain has a lever of checks and balances to help us respond appropriately to what is going on around us. A threat to our safety results in our "alarm center" telling the hypothalamus to tell the pituitary to tell the adrenal gland to release the stress hormones adrenaline and cortisol. Physiologically we are then equipped to fight against the threat if we believe we can overcome it, or flee from it if we can't. People who have lived under excessive stress for any reason are more likely to have the alarm center firing off inappropriately. In this setting the stress hormones are not really needed; consequently, the person experiences symptoms of anxiety and stress along with unwelcome physiological reactions to the extra adrenaline.

Recently I asked Fred what the most stress-free time of his life was. He thought for a moment, then said, "Before I married you."

"Ha ha. And the second-most stress-free time?"

He readily acknowledged that the slower-paced, uncomplicated lifestyle of the "Friendly Faces, Beautiful Places" state provoked a most soothing state of mind.

A few years ago we both had Carolina on our minds, so we visited the old neighborhood and old friends. It felt the same, y'all.

Healing Words

"Therefore, each of you must put off falsehood and speak truthfully to his neighbor, for we are all members of one body."
Ephesians 4:25

Our fear of rejection, lack of understanding about our own fears and anxiety, and our inability to trust God can cause us to wear a mask. As long as we wear masks, our progress toward spiritual, mental, and emotional maturity will be thwarted, as well as our ability to achieve intimacy in relationships.

"He who gets wisdom loves his own soul; he who cherishes understanding prospers." Proverbs 19:8

Sometimes, wisdom's best teacher is experience. Through experiences we can learn to be attuned and sensitive to our God-given strengths and weaknesses. Our suffering is reduced and our lives are enriched.

4

Don't Be Happy . . . Worry!

How far you go in life depends on your being tender with the young, compassionate with the aged, sympathetic with the striving, and tolerant of the weak and the strong. Because some day in life you will have been all of these.

George Washington Carver

One day I looked around at the women I knew and decided that they all had low self-esteem. So I planned a women's seminar at our church to give them a boost. The title was "Bettering Your Balance." Because I was in performance mode, I deluded myself. I thought that with a small committee's help, I could put this on in a few months. I expected an audience in the thousands. I expected thunder and applause. I expected lives to be changed forever. One was—mine.

Southern Fried Chick

Three weeks before the seminar, Fred, the kids, and I traveled to Ohio for our yearly visit. I worried all the way about this enormous burden I had taken on, even though I'd left the details in the hands of a committee. Trips stressed me out anyway. I was never comfortable outside of my own environment, and Fred always pressured the kids and me to keep the car neat; he was a literal litter sergeant.

As soon as we were on our way, I would close my eyes and try to rest, but I could never fall asleep–I was too nervous and edgy. Nervous exhaustion was much worse than physical exhaustion. With nervous exhaustion I couldn't sleep because my brain was too keyed up. The problem compounded itself until I was hardly functional. And I was so embarrassed at feeling like a wimp that I tried to conceal the problem, which took even more energy. At least when I'm physically exhausted, sleep comes easily. Mental stress is a killer.

After arriving home from each vacation, my brain needed a month to decelerate from its high anxiety level. Picture your car stuck in first gear with the motor running, and you can't turn off the ignition or put the car in neutral or park. I would lie idling on the couch for days after coming home, doing the bare minimum to maintain the household.

This most recent trip to my parents' was the worst. The first night there I had a major, full-blown anxiety attack—somewhat different from a classic panic attack—not as intense, but lasting a lot longer. I was in bed in the middle of the night, heart racing, negative thoughts putting my mind into a frenzy, as total despair and hopelessness engulfed me for endless hours. A)

The first night back in Atlanta I sensed another anxiety attack coming on. I got out of bed and went into my son's upper bunk. I decided Fred was the enemy and causing half my problems and I would spend the rest of my married life sleeping in James' bunk bed. This was probably the worst and best night of my thirty-nine-year-old life. The worst because of the intensity of the mental anguish . . . the best because, deep in my gut, I knew there was hope. But first I was going to have to get mad.

In my mixed emotional state of hopefulness and anger, I determined I would never have another anxiety/panic attack. Too painful. I didn't know how I would keep from having another attack, I just knew I would. Climbing up out of the abyss and forging a path to emotional wholeness wouldn't be easy, but I would try.

I made a mental note to concentrate on *me* after the seminar. I was slowly but surely taking responsibility for my problems. I learned mental healing wasn't a straight shot, like getting an injection of penicillin for an infection. There was some zigging and zagging, and I took numerous detours along the path, but I made major strides in communication,

---

A) An anxiety or panic attack floods the system with adrenaline or other alarm-type chemicals. These attacks cause such fear and discomfort that a person becomes terrified of having more attacks, putting the nervous system at "high alert" status, and setting the stage for more outpouring of alarm chemicals. A vicious cycle is then set up where anxiety breeds more anxiety.

awareness, and understanding—all part of the recovery process. Amazingly, my kids never seemed affected by my bizarre behavior. Maybe they naïvely thought that all moms laid on the couch for days after a vacation. I was still meeting the kids' needs, though barely. All my energy was concentrated on them, even though helping with something as simple as a fifth grade reading project was extremely painful.

As my "Bettering Your Balance" seminar neared, I continued to worry and lose balance. Only seven women initially signed up, meaning I was a few thousand women short of my projection. Ironically, the scripture verse we chose as the seminar theme was, "For God has not given you a spirit of fear, but of power, and of love, and of a sound mind" (2Timothy 1:7, KJV).[1]

Another problem: Our church could not host the seminar as planned, because the restroom plumbing broke. I tried to think of creative solutions to the problem. Offering *Depends* to the women was probably not an option. Or perhaps I could change the title from "Bettering Your Balance" to "Bettering Your Bladder."

The seminar, held in a middle school, was a huge success, and not only because the toilets flushed. I flushed too—several of the original seven women plus seventy more who showed up were effusive in their praise of the speakers and the program.

As the program coordinator and emcee, I had fooled everyone with my fake self confidence, even though I was running on empty and exhausted to the point of collapse. I came home relieved the seminar was successful, but still couldn't shut off the anxiety.

The next morning, a Sunday, I wanted to stay in bed, fetal position, with the sheet pulled over my nose. Fred insisted I go to church, so I did—drained and anxious.

After the service, our assistant pastor noticed my frazzled state. He confided in me about his own panic disorder, and that he was seeing a psychiatrist. I was stunned. I thought pastors bypassed mental problems. He also recommended *I* get help, as he recognized my symptoms. I felt ashamed and pooh-pooed the idea, knowing that once I recovered from this episode I would be just fine.

Shame on me and woe was me for not immediately taking that first step to getting help. I thought I could bounce back on my own if I prayed hard enough or used enough willpower. I had no idea that my imbalanced brain chemistry was underlying my problems.

I was one of the masses suffering from depression or anxiety who didn't know they needed professional help. How *do* you know when you need help? Do you make an appointment after two anxiety attacks? Three? What's the cut off? Do you wait until you're spending all day in bed in a fetal position? What are the telltale signs?

Diane Hales and Robert E. Hales, M.D., authors of *Caring for the Mind* (Bantam), suggest: *". . . think about how intensely a problem is affecting you or a loved one and how long it has lasted. If the difficulty is causing great distress and interfering with work, relationships or other aspects of life, it is wise to seek help. What distinguishes mental disorders from problems of daily living is their severity or persistence over time."*

The Rhythm Method

While I was busy getting wound tighter than a top, Fred was busy reading about circadian rhythm (how our body clocks operate with our sleep-wake cycle). He said waking up at the same time every morning would fix my problems. He was adamant, so I attempted the circadian rhythm thing. Even if a person went to bed late at night, she was supposed to rise at the same time every morning. (For those of you who need your sleep, isn't that a *hilarious* thought?) B)

I tried this circadian rhythm thing on our next trip to see if it would help my anxiety. The rhythm method failed. My anxiety was so bad I was using sleeping pills every night, I had chronic heart palpitations and was full of fear, mainly because I knew I was going to fail at circadian rhythm, and I hated to fail. I had a better idea, though; I confided in an equally fragile friend. She offered me a few of her Xanax tranquilizers, which I stashed in my purse. C)

B) Circadian rhythm refers to the body's built-in clock. Sleep-wake patterns, body temperature, and production of cortisol are all regulated by the body's built-in clock system, or circadian rhythm. Our twenty-four-hour clocks are controlled by the pineal gland, which secretes melatonin, the body clock regulator. If the light-dark, sleep-wake systems are out of sync, a person is more vulnerable to a predisposition towards any psychiatric illness.

C) Sharing drugs is a common and dangerous practice. People vary tremendously in their responses to medication; how fast the medication is absorbed and metabolized, etc. A medication may work for one person but may have undesirable effects for another. The narcissistic myth goes: "If it's good for me, it's good for anyone else." This is a commonly held—and hazardous—belief.

Debugging by the Book

Once home, I went to the library to pick up books on anxiety. I wanted some tools to help me deal with this giant bug in my brain. I checked out a book called *Women and Anxiety*[2] that offered several steps to resolution:

"These steps can help you expose the conflicts that create anxiety and lead to stumbling blocks in your relationships, your work, and your general progress. . . . You can learn, too, how to try to strengthen qualities that are lying dormant within you and can give you new hope."

Here were some of the steps I took towards new hope:

Select a single troublesome issue that causes you to feel anxious, or that creates repeated tension, guilt, anger, or conflict.
Going on trips, with (or without) Fred, makes me feel anxious and concerned.

Determine how [this issue] is causing you or someone else to suffer.
Whenever I am anxious I tend to lose sleep, which often causes more anxiety and causes Fred to be totally annoyed and creates tension in the family.

State whether or not you have tried to disregard the issue.
In some ways, yes, by denying that it's going to happen again, and having a false belief that I'm "cured."

State whether or not you have tried to deal with the issue.
Yes, by praying, by keeping a list of things to be done before we go, by trying to communicate with Fred.

Decide why your efforts at solution have not been effective.
Mainly due to Fred's lack of encouragement. His negative comments make me even more anxious as I feel, "Yes, he's right. I am going to be a basket case."

Find out how you react to change in regard to that issue.
Can Fred change? Either himself, or his view of me? Would he recognize a "reformed zucchini" if he saw one? ("Zucchini" being Fred's pet name for me while I'm in a vegetative state.)

Enumerate what you can lose and what you can gain by making a change in the issue you've selected.
Nothing to lose. What's to gain? Good memories of fun activities and conversations, a richer life, peace.

Choose a possible solution in dealing with the issue.
Ask Fred if he loves me unconditionally, and even if I was a basket case on the next trip, would he still love me? I would feel more secure if I knew the answer was yes.

We had been home one day when I decided to make an appointment with a psychologist. My anxiety was no better. I remembered the Xanax-on-loan however, and decided to try half a pill. Within a half-hour my heart palpitations and worrying stopped; I was calm, I had energy, and could think clearly. I still made the appointment.

All Shook Up

During that brief time of so-called clarity and energy, I decided to throw Fred a surprise birthday party with an Elvis theme. It's possible the Xanax put me in a temporary false state of calm, self confidence, and forgetfulness.

I forgot that Fred hates parties. He would rather have a barium enema than be around large groups of people, especially when he's the main attraction. Perhaps there was a manic side to this anxiety. I've heard of manic depression, but manic anxiety? I wonder if Elvis ever took Xanax when he was all shook up.

This party decision slowed my progress. I had felt a slight bit less anxious, and thought I would continue to make steady improvement, regardless of my bad choices.

People responded to the party invitation about the time I ran out of Xanax. Suddenly I didn't want to throw a party. I wanted to throw up. I could have canceled, but I would have considered myself a failure. Luckily I had the appointment with the psychologist two days before the party, and I knew she would have instant answers. (I never told Fred that I had made the appointment. I was afraid he would keep me from going. My willingness to be transparent with Fred was a work in progress.)

I don't even remember what I told the psychologist. I think I rambled in disconnected sentences. She appeared to be caring, but said little, other than that she thought I had panic disorder and needed to be on Prozac, and Ativan—a tranquilizer. She said she would confer with the psychiatrist on staff and call in the prescriptions. I told her I would think about the drugs. *Boy, I'm worse off than I thought . . . she wants to put me on* **two** *drugs! Wow . . . I really* **am** *crazy!*

I learned that it's fairly common to feel worse initially, after a *You're Really Not OK* diagnosis. The reality hits: *I'm clinically depressed and have papers to prove it. And now I have to see a counselor and take pills.*

Also, I was taken aback that the psychiatrist himself didn't see me. Wouldn't he need to evaluate me before passing out drugs? Apparently not, although I knew he must sign the prescription. Psychologists cannot prescribe medication.

Meanwhile, Fred's surprise party was a day away, and I was becoming an emotional wreck. I reluctantly called the psychologist and requested the prescription for Prozac, not understanding that antidepressants take at least two weeks to have an effect, according to my contributor Dr. James Mallory. By the morning of the party, it struck me that I probably needed the tranquilizer, so I called the psychologist for the Ativan prescription.

The Elvis party was a hit for everyone but me. At one time during the evening I ran in the closet to have a panic attack, but was able to abort the worst of it with an Ativan. By 11:00 that night I was fried. I came downstairs in my pajamas and told my guests the Elvis party was over—I was going to bed. After everyone left I took another Ativan and waited for sleep.

The Elvis episode, and this chapter, are now over.

Thank you, thank you very much.

Healing Words

"For he has not despised or disdained the suffering of the afflicted one; he has not hidden his face from him but has listened to his cry for help." Psalms 22:24

We rarely feel like God is listening to us when we're in a state of utter despair. Thankfully, God hears our prayers regardless of how we feel, honoring the tiniest shred of faith as we humbly seek Him.

"Blessed is the man who finds wisdom, the man who gains under-standing, for she is more profitable than silver and yields better returns than gold . . . her ways are pleasant ways, and all her paths are peace." Proverbs 3:13-14, 17

When we gain a measure of wisdom, we will also gain a measure of peace; the two go hand in hand.

5

Getting My God Fix

We want lives of simple, predictable ease—smooth, even trails as far as the eye can see—but God likes to go off-road.

Tony Snow, former White House Press Secretary

It was a Sunday morning, the day after the Elvis party. Fred and the kids were up and I was still in bed, fetal position, head buried in the pillow, sheet over my nose with just my darting eyes peering out. I somewhat resembled a terrorized Middle Eastern woman being smothered in a bleached burka.

The Hollywood Church

I didn't want to go to church that morning, but Fred insisted I go—not, however, to our regular church with him and the kids. He wanted me to go to a church he called the Hollywood Church, because of all the cameras and monitors. Fred had visited one time and said he felt something. He thought I needed to feel something too.

Fred and the kids left for church. I roused myself and called a friend for a ride to the Hollywood Church. On the way, I had heart palpitations and felt an overall sense of foreboding; similar to the feeling I had about throwing my babies out the window when they were newborns.

My friend and I reached our pew as the choir sang. Fred was right. I was feeling something. I determined it was God seeping under my scared skin. My heart palpitations slowed. The music and worship were unlike anything I had ever experienced. At this point, the pastor hadn't said a word. In fact, I don't remember anything the pastor said that morning. I just remember feeling something.

My "feeling something" provoked a rather dramatic transformation during that ninety-minute service. I walked in weak, frazzled, and frightened, but I walked out totally at peace. This peace, though temporary, was a powerful and significant step forward.

I immediately decided to go off the Prozac, after being on it for a mere ten days. The stuff was giving me stomach cramps. Besides, God had healed me.

At my follow-up appointment with the psychologist the next week, I told her I went off the Prozac because God had healed me at the Hollywood Church. We agreed that since God took care of the problem, I needed no more appointments. She wished me well and I never saw her again.

The Hollywood Church continued to be a wonderful, worshipful experience. The music and praise, especially, soothed my jangled inner-jumpiness.

On the Sunday mornings when I felt troubled, I would go to the altar for a spiritual lube job. The elders anointed me with oil and prayed for me. And I would feel better, until the next Sunday.

Getting My God Fix

The worship service was like getting a weekly and powerful injection of God into my brain. Fred called it "my fix," but he couldn't deny that I had changed. The church "embraced me at my point of need and led me into the presence of Christ . . ." which just happens to be its mission statement.

The music, the uplifting message, and the prayers were all crucial to helping me attain at least a temporary peace of mind. I could fend off for another week the anxiety tentacles crouching in the crevices of my cranium.

From a sermon at the Hollywood Church, I learned that singing praises to God can bring healing, deliverance, and restoration. Mental health clinics, not especially known for being spiritual havens, are also aware of the restorative power of music. Ridgeview Institute in Atlanta, for instance, incorporates inspirational music into its stress reduction programs.

I tend to prefer—even to crave—lively praise songs set to upbeat music. But maybe some old biddy gets equally charged up singing a sixteenth century hymn that needs Cliff Notes to explain it. One day *I'll* be that old biddy singin' the defunct ditty.

When I hear a motivational, uplifting speaker, preacher, teacher, or music, I just feel *good*. My psychiatrist contributor Dr. Mallory says that's partly due to my serotonin levels rising in response. Serotonin is a calming brain chemical that, in the right amounts, makes for a happy brain. The now happy brain causes a change in the person's mood, which causes a change in behavior, and lives and relationships are ultimately enriched. A)

Personally, my serotonin levels have never increased upon hearing "pond scum" sermons: those that address the congregation as depraved humanity, allowed to live and breathe by God's grace alone. Apparently (and inexplicably) some seminaries teach "Pond Scum 101" as part of their course material. I prefer what I call "power" preaching that strengthens and challenges me. Pond scum preaching weakens and depresses me. My mind and spirit cannot bear hearing about a wrathful God from the pulpit, when wrath alone is the theme. More than anything else, I believe God is merciful—and mercy triumphs over judgment. *Praise Jay-sus.*

A Self-Help Smorgasbord

On Wednesday nights I attended every self-help group that the church offered. Professional Christian therapists affiliated with a local counseling center led many of the groups. The topics ranged from depression and anxiety, to codependency, compulsive eating, and assertiveness.

Every group session always left me feeling helped and encouraged. I did skip some groups however, like the "Living Stones," which ministered to recovering gay people. Although I must confess, I was a lesbian for about forty-five minutes when I was eleven. This preadolescent experiment/experience is probably not all that uncommon.

A) Serotonin is one of the most important neurotransmitters in the brain. Imbalances in serotonin are involved in anxiety, depression, panic disorder, and obsessive-compulsive disorder, as well as in certain eating disorders, and probably in some addictions.

One night I even went to a "Divorce Recovery" group. I've never been divorced, but I took a friend who needed a ride. I had a great time, did a lot of talking, and found out that many divorced people go through depression and anxiety on top of the grief that comes with losing a spouse.

Naturally, the weekly anxiety sessions interested me more than any other. I enjoyed the great camaraderie, sitting in a room with other people who had bugs in their brains. One could say the room was bugged. During these sessions we learned about the several causes of anxiety: psychological causes like fears, conflicts, unmet needs; and physical causes that included pre-existing physical illnesses and chemical imbalances. B)

The Wednesday night sessions also focused on anxiety's *effects*.

The physical:

- Heart palpitations
- Restlessness
- Insomnia
- Inability to focus

And the relational:

- Dealing with an anxious person's agitated state
- Withdrawal from friends and family

The teaching concluded with some remedies for overcoming anxiety:

- Face our fears
- Develop a more peaceful environment
- Change our thoughts and close out the past

The information in these sessions was good, but I realized that overcoming and managing anxiety would be hard work unless God planned to hit the class with a bug zapper, instantaneously healing us. I wondered if

---

B) Virtually all psychiatric conditions involve an imbalance of one or more of these chemical systems in the brain: neurotransmitters, hormones, endorphins, chemicals produced by stress, as well as other complicated systems. What causes the imbalance is not always known. Genetics, psychological and physical trauma, medication, infections, and brain damage are all known to play a role in chemical alterations.

God would zap me. I pictured him on a movie screen as Luke Skywalker, healing us with a simple "bzzzzzzt" of his white, bug-zapping laser gun. Out with *Star Wars*, in with new title: *Holy War on Brain Bugs*, with the subtitle: *It's a Bug's Death*. But I digress.

No Groupie Left Behind?

Some Wednesday Night Groupies seemed stuck in park, and I hoped I wouldn't become one of them. They were happy to be labeled as depressed, codependent, etc. They could come to these wonderful group meetings week after week, get their brains massaged, and never deal with the pain of growing and healing. I also wondered how the leaders dealt with the members who refused to "graduate" with the rest of their class, showing up instead for the next session, and the next, and the next.

Don't "Off" the Zoloft

When I was in the depths of my chemical imbalance—usually between Sunday mornings during my initial visits to the Hollywood Church—compassionate friends prayed for my healing. But when I revealed to them some victory, like lowering the dose of my medication, they acted *overly* relieved and happy, almost as though I had gotten rid of a demon. I could tell that some of them really wanted me off this stuff.

As I look back years later, I realize those well-meaning friends who had a problem with my taking medication had blind spots about their caffeine, alcohol, shopping, nicotine, food, and relationship addictions. But none of my friends judged me for using Zoloft, or any other antidepressant I took over the years. They just wanted me off that stuff because none of them had any experience with—or knowledge of—antidepressants; therefore the drug must be dangerous. What was dangerous was me *without* the Zoloft.

Anxiety Aerobics

I continued recovering, but one thing still bugged me. From time to time I had insomnia, and I'd take a mild tranquilizer. Yet I felt so guilty and ashamed about taking this little white half-of-a-pill that I hid my embarrassing habit from Fred.

Some nights I'd get up and eat a cheese sandwich, Fred's recommendation for insomnia. Fred was always recommending something: circadian rhythm, cheese sandwich, bran pills, magnets, or drinking olive oil.

My insomnia/anxiety usually happened in the middle of the night. I'd awaken with heart palpitations and attempt to calm down with muscle-relaxing exercises. I started with my feet, tensing and releasing my toes, but not for long. I always developed painful toe cramps, causing me to thrash around wildly—but quietly—so as not to wake Fred. So I'd give up the muscle relaxing and go to deep breathing. But I was so traumatized by the toe cramps that the deep breathing turned into hyperventilating. So now I'm back to heart palpitations. This is where I began quoting the twenty-third psalm: "The Lord is my Shepherd, I shall not want [heart palpitations] . . ." If that didn't work I'd start counting backwards, beginning at 10,000.

When I finally gave up the anxiety ritual, I groped for the pill. Often I couldn't find it. Sometimes I'd knock a book off the night stand while searching and Fred would hear a "boom!" I covered up the sound by coughing or changing position in bed, and hoped that Fred might think he was dreaming about Vietnam. (Fred was never in 'Nam, but he pretends he was.) Every time I went through this ritual I suffered guilt and shame that I actually had to take a drug. But I tried to forget and pretend everything was OK. After all, I was healed, wasn't I? God wouldn't let me down, would He?

I lacked the self-awareness or knowledge to know that I was in the early stages of recovery. I thought I was ready to reclaim full control of my life. I considered myself healed, delivered, kaput, the end. What did happen is that God met me at my point of need and ministered to me. He didn't heal me. If He had, this book would be a very short story. So the bad news: God didn't heal me; the process continues. The good news: You get to read the rest of my book.

Healing Words

David said to God, "I am in deep distress. Let us fall into the hands of the Lord, for his mercy is great; but do not let me fall into the hands of men." 2 Samuel 24:14

David knew, as we do, that God is more merciful to us than we are to each other. When in deep distress, there is no better place for us to fall than into God's arms.

"No discipline seems pleasant at the time, but painful. Later on, however, it produces a harvest of righteousness and peace for those who have been trained by it." Hebrews 12:1

Our journeys towards healing are just that: journeys. We may take two steps forward and one step back, but the goal is to keep moving forward with the end in mind—which is peace of mind. It's well worth the effort.

Dear Shelley:

Thank you for your letter and tremendous testimony of God's healing in your life. I rejoice with you and pray that your healing will be complete in every way.

May God bless you as you continue to grow in your relationship with Him.

Sincerely,

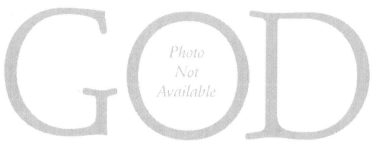

BUT THAT'S OK WITH

GOD

Photo
Not
Available

Finding the Humor and Healing in Life

6

Help! My Brain Has Fallen and It Can't Get Up!

After the Resurrection, our bodies will be perfect. We'll be so happy we won't care what happens to our brains.

Sister Nicolette Welter, who is part of a study that uses the brains of deceased nuns for research to probe the causes of Alzheimer's disease.

Early spring ushers in the most beautiful yet aggravating time of year to Atlanta. The dogwoods are in full bloom, and the thick pollen paints a yellow coat over the landscape. By late March, the surroundings look slightly jaundiced. The pollen permeates homes, casting yellow particles everywhere, and causing some type of discomfort to almost everyone.

Fortunately, the pollen doesn't bother me, but I'm still having an allergic reaction—to myself. I don't like me. For supposed fun, I'm playing a few sets of doubles tennis with several neighborhood women. But I'm not having fun. My team is losing four games out of five. We alternate players, but I am the jinx for both teams. I am a loser. I feel like I'm in junior high, Section Eight. The women don't seem to care about winning or losing. They're laughing and having fun. What's wrong with them? What's wrong with me?

I recognize these early warning signs of depression—the negative, intrusive thoughts, irritability, and worthless feelings—but I continue to be in denial at the same time. I want to believe so badly that I'm over this mental junk. The insomnia returns, so I take my tranquilizer again at night. Problem: I am about to run out and have no refill on my prescription because I hadn't seen the psychologist in over a year. The last time I saw her, I gave her my victorious testimony of healing. I'm functional, but fragile, and fading by the minute.

How to Be a Host When You Feel Like Toast

Fred and I had been attending a couples' Bible study in our neighbor-hood. Each week we went to a different home, where invariably the wife served up a delectable smorgasbord, straight out of the pages of a *Southern Living* cookbook. I found the outlay of food to be a bit over the top; I knew how much work was involved with cleaning and cooking. The food didn't seem necessary, especially since we always met after dinner. I dreaded my turn, as now I would have to perform to keep up with my neighbors. I absolutely did not have the emotional or physical energy required to entertain anything but thoughts of sheer panic. I felt like I was on the reality show *Hell's Kitchen,* only more hellish. In my *Hell's Kitchen,* the evil chef screamed because I was just standing there—not even making an effort to prepare a dish that would ultimately taste like crap. Fortunately a neighbor rescued me and prepared hors d'oeuvres. Between my neighbor and the cleaning lady, I pulled it off.

As I get older, I have less inclination (and energy) to impress women. And I'm certainly not trying to impress the *men* who come to our home. Men-people won't even notice the dust on top of my refrigerator. And if they do notice, they still won't care. That's one of the things I admire about men—they just don't care—except about the important stuff like food, sex, and college football.

About 10:30 that night, our group study still going strong, I got a long distance call from my mom, who told me that my cousin Mark had committed suicide. He was twenty-seven, schizophrenic, and a Christian. He was doing well, we thought. He lived in California in a supervised home and had a job. I was stunned.

1-800-ANX-IOUS

After everyone left, my thoughts raced: *But Mark was doing so well . . . we had such hope for him . . . the reports were good . . . his future looked promising. Oh my God, am I next? I thought I was doing well; will I eventually kill myself like Mark did?* My warped, exhausted brain identified with Mark, even though I wasn't schizophrenic and my circumstances were different.

I stayed awake all night pondering what to do about my mental condition. The next morning I found this ad in the newspaper:

ANXIOUS? Free Medical Treatment is Available!
Look for these symptoms:

- Palpitations or racing heart
- Dizziness or lightheadedness
- Shaking or trembling
- Hot and cold flashes
- Lack of energy or tiring easily
- Difficulty concentrating
- Shortness of breath
- Smothering or choking sensations
- Nausea or diarrhea
- Difficulty sleeping
- Constant worrying
- Uncontrollable panicky feelings

If you suffer from three or more of the above, you may benefit from free treatment that includes strict medical supervision, physical examinations, lab tests, EKGs, and new medications. The entire program is FREE OF CHARGE! *Call I-800-"ANX-IOUS" for more information.*

I called and told the woman almost proudly that I had all but four of the symptoms, and then asked her what I needed to do to sign up. She told me that they were a medical research center given funds by drug companies to test various medications on willing participants. Certain people were given placebos and others were given the actual drug over several weeks. I said to her, "Are you telling me, when I am suffering from all but four of these anxiety symptoms I might be given a *placebo* over several weeks? I may be nuts, but I'm not stupid!"

I couldn't believe that people suffering from high anxiety would become guinea pigs. However, I now understand that each situation is different. Many mentally ill people can be taken advantage of and thus are quite vulnerable. Lacking money for regular psychiatric care motivates them to join an experiment. I was fortunate enough to have money for *real* treatment, so I skipped the study and made an appointment with a counseling center. I told Fred about the appointment and was surprised that he agreed I should go, although he still didn't understand my problem.

My tranquilizer stash was completely out, so I attempted to make an appointment for the next week. I was told I must see the psychiatrist first, as he prescribed any medication. But his next available appointment was six weeks away. "Can't wait that long," I begged. "I need the med *now!*" I was squeezed in for the following week to see both the psychologist and the psychiatrist.

Another week of sleepless nights, but at least I had hope that I would soon be out of my misery. I was thankful that I never lost my faith when I was so mentally miserable. I doubted and wavered, but decided against becoming an agnostic or atheist. Then *all* hope would be lost.

A few years earlier I had started a graphic design business—which I loved—until my anxiety disorder did a hostile takeover in '92. I was barely able to keep the business going. I took calls while lying on the floor of my home office, enduring tension headaches every day for three months.

During this tense time I had two difficult clients. I was producing an employee handbook and newsletter for one client who was in over her head. I was in over her head too, and mine. We made quite a team. My client was educated beyond her intelligence, ineptly handling a position of responsibility and authority. I dealt with her daily for two months. Thankfully, I had developed enough assertiveness to tell my difficult clients they couldn't walk all over me. Well, actually they could have since I was always laid out on the floor.

Diagnosis: You're Not OK, But at Least You're Not Stupid

The day of my appointment at the counseling center, I put on make up and contact lenses for the first time in weeks. I met with the psychologist for an hour. A) He took a family history and I told him what I was doing in order to deal with my anxiety: going to church, getting prayed over, meditating on various scriptures, exercising, avoiding caffeine after noon, simplifying life, and educating myself on anxiety. He told me how unusual my efforts were, that only a tiny three percent of patients actually tried to rid themselves of mental distress prior to their first visit. He briefly assessed my situation as "a kind of anxiety disorder accompanied by mild depression," but said the psychiatrist would give a more official diagnosis.

He then told me something I will never forget. No one had ever told me this before or since, I might add. He said "Shelley, I believe you are highly intelligent." I was so stunned I was momentarily speechless. When I finally spoke I said, weakly, "No, I'm not." But he insisted that I was. I

A) Through counseling, the patient is able to ventilate all the hurts locked up inside without receiving rejection. One is able to identify and clarify all the ins and outs of conflicts. A plan of action to bring change is developed. Counseling benefits the patient by helping him/her get out from under the sense of being overwhelmed, while promoting the process of healing.

tried again to tell the guy I wasn't a rocket scientist, but I couldn't convince him I was anything less than highly intelligent. I then decided he was probably the most brilliant man I had ever met. I agreed to make another appointment to find out what other fascinating insights he had. I walked out of his office feeling, well, highly intelligent in a mentally disheveled sort of way.

The Doctor Is In and He Is Cute!

From the counselor's office I walked into the psychiatrist's office and instantly developed a crush on him. Dr. C. looked like Jon Voight the actor, was as tall as Fred (6'4-1/2"), had a kind face and slightly unruly gray hair, which I found charming. I'd been married for thirteen years, and I still found Fred quite handsome. So what was up with my growing attraction to the shrink? Well I'll tell you what was up.

When one spouse (me) does not have a mate (him) blessed with an ear for compassion or understanding, and someone of the opposite sex gives that spouse attention, the vulnerable spouse (still me) can misread the attention and be tempted to start a relationship. If the party giving the attention is also open to temptation, you have a mangled marriage in the making. (Maybe two.)

This is not what happened in my case, but I can see how easily it might. People in the "listening" professions, such as psychiatrists, psychologists, pastors, counselors, and doctors, have to guard against compromising their ethics and professional standards. The good-looking ones need to be especially careful. But, on second thought, maybe looks aren't critical—perhaps we weak ones would find a lizard attractive if he/she gave us their undivided attention and took notes while we talked.

I nervously rattled off my life story at breakneck speed. Dr. C. wrote while nodding his head and interjecting questions. He asked me if I exercised (besides my mouth, I assumed) and I told him that I walked at least thirty minutes a day and had been walking for years. He said that wasn't enough exercise for me and then asked if I could jog. I told him that I had occasionally managed three miles and he said, "Good, you need to do it." He then told me about an obsessive-compulsive patient who alleviated his symptoms by running ten miles a day.

At the end of the session the doctor said: "I don't believe you have panic disorder. I would call it atypical anxiety disorder." After a few more sessions he modified his diagnosis to generalized anxiety disorder (GAD).

GAD All Over

The National Institute for Mental Health describes GAD as much more than the typical worrying your grandmother does. It's chronic and exaggerated worry and tension with no discernible cause. GADders always feel uneasy and apprehensive, and sometimes have trouble falling or staying asleep.[1] Physical symptoms include sweaty palms, nausea, increased heart rate, trembling, twitching, tension headaches, and irritability. We have trouble concentrating, are easily fatigued, and sometimes suffer from depression as well. GAD is known to start in childhood, and affects women more than men.[2]

After Dr. C. made his diagnosis, he then asked about my medication history. I told him about my experience with stomach cramps while taking Prozac. He said, "Have you ever heard of Desyrel, a long-distance cousin of Prozac? Desyrel has the added benefit of causing sleepiness." *Yeah right . . . general anesthesia wouldn't put me under, considering the high red alert state I'm in.* He also prescribed a tranquilizer and said he wanted to see me in two weeks.

Within several days I began to feel the positive effects from the antidepressant. With the added benefit of the tranquilizer, I was finally falling and staying asleep. I told myself that I would not suffer any more mental torment and would take whatever drugs I needed to avoid further pain. Although I was exhausted, I made myself jog for three miles a few times a week, which did help my mental state. But I hated the jogging—no endorphins ever kicked in—so as soon as I felt better, I began aerobic walking with a friend.

I saw the counselor for five more sessions. He originally said I would probably need fifteen to twenty sessions. But I'm somewhat of a tightwad, and therapy sessions weren't cheap. I figured I could easily whittle down the number from twenty to five, especially if I talked fast, which I did.

During the counseling sessions, we discussed my entire history of angst and how I found it difficult to confront people who irritated or annoyed me, or—in the current vernacular—"crossed my boundaries." I had no problem with professional business relationships. But personal relationships affected me more . . . personally. I felt guilty expressing my negative feelings to acquaintances and friends, and turned such feelings inward. I learned from the counselor that I couldn't afford to do that. Holding in feelings leads to incapacitating anxiety for a person with my genetic makeup and temperament. In summary, I quit fearing rejection, and learned to express anger in a healthy way; at least that was the plan.

Once I realized expressing anger is OK, even *essential* for my mental wellbeing, I no longer worried so much about others' reactions. I started confronting people. If you offended me, you heard about it. My new approach was quite healing for me, but those who knew me were taken aback, especially Fred. He kept asking me if I had PMS. I did attempt to be tactful, but I'm sure I failed initially. Bungling confrontations are to be expected when anger has been bottled for years.

I'm convinced that my fear of rejection was a major reason for my anxiety disorder. The freedom of being able to speak the truth without the fear of rejection getting in the way, was . . . well, freeing.

Another wonderful discovery: It's OK to fail, and even necessary if I wanted to succeed. I had been so concerned with my reputation that I felt everything I did must be successful. In *Gone With the Wind*, Rhett Butler advises Scarlett O'Hara: "With enough courage my dear, you don't need a reputation." Risking failure takes courage, especially when people are watching. I needed to stop looking at my mistakes as failures.

Funny Thing About Laughter . . .

Laughter is not only good for the soul, but it's a great elixir for the mind and body as well. Call it aerobic exercise for the innards. I haven't known many mental health professionals who laughed. They'd feel better if they did, and they'd certainly put their patients more at ease by using appropriate humor.

Norman Cousin's book, *Anatomy of an Illness* (Bantam Books), discusses the healing power of humor. Recovering from a crippling spinal disease, the author watched reruns of Marx Brothers movies and Candid Camera videos as part of his therapy. Cousins reported that twenty minutes of hearty laughter brought him two hours of painless sleep.

My good friend "Betty" snapped herself out of several weeks of depression through laughter. Betty's husband "Joe" continually schemes and plans ways to get rich quick. His hypomanic mind rapid fires from one hot deal to another. Whenever he strikes a new deal, he tells Betty, "In a few months I'll be making seven figures . . . we won't have any financial worries the rest of our lives." Meanwhile, Betty fears loss of their cars and utilities for nonpayment. Not only were Betty and Joe in a constant money pit, but Betty was in a pit of depression. Joe's latest hot deal, something about "buying an island in the Caribbean and renting out penthouse suites," was so ludicrous that Betty laughed in the midst of her depression. And the more Joe talked, the more Betty laughed until she cried. She actually felt the veil of depression being lifted. Meanwhile, her husband cursed at her for laughing at him, but she didn't care. Laughter prevailed over lunacy.

I've learned to use humor in unorthodox settings. While giving the eulogy at my mother-in-law's funeral, I told the mourners, "We are burying Grandma in her long underwear . . . one of her rules was to wear her Long John's until June and, since this is May, they're going with her." The responses were interesting to watch. A few people bent the corners of their lips, others chortled and chuckled, but some looked like I'd committed some sacrilege. The sacrilege would have been to *not* bury Grandma in her long underwear.

A great outcome of the therapy, drugs, and reading was that I began arguing with Fred. I didn't realize marriage could be so animated and fun. I sometimes yelled at Fred to make my point, but at least I was communicating—actually I was fighting for a better marriage. Fred caught my drift and we quit drifting apart.

Since things were going well, I weaned myself off the antidepressant Desyrel, which I had been taking for eighteen months. Besides, Dr. C. had implied that a year's worth of medication was plenty. B) I encouraged

---

B) Most psychiatrists now believe that nine months is not just the minimum time to be on antidepressants, but the minimum time a person should be totally out of depression before considering coming off the medication. This is true only for those having their first attack of depression. If a person has had three or more separate depressive attacks, most psychiatrists will recommend an indefinite regimen of antidepressants.

myself with: *"Maybe my brain is back for good."*

Maybe I was wrong.

Wino's Guide to Jogging

I was also wrong to fly Fred and me to West Palm Beach for his birthday. I thought maybe I could handle the trip. I couldn't. Negative "trip" memories were still taunting and haunting my subconscious. I didn't sleep the night before we left or the two nights in the hotel. In fact, I stayed drunk the whole time. I was out of my tranquilizers. And I hadn't bothered to fill the prescription, thinking I was through with medication. My alternatives to medication were wine and jogging—two things I knew from experience that would relieve anxiety—albeit temporarily.

To calm my frazzled nerves, I drank a bottle of Chablis wine and we found a park where I jogged for a couple of miles. I kind of wove from side to side, because I was drunk. The trip was a disaster for me, but Fred said he enjoyed himself. I couldn't wait to come home to my own bed. Took me a couple nights to wind down from my downed wine.

Healing Words

". . . a time to weep and a time to laugh." Ecclesiastes 3:4

The time to weep and the time to laugh can be almost one and the same time. Laughter helps heal our hurts, offers us happy memories in the midst of pain, and draws us closer together in the face of grief.

"Pride goes before destruction, a haughty spirit before a fall."
Proverbs 16:18-19

Sometimes we fail to respect our God-given limitations. We take on too much, too fast, and then suffer the consequences, such as a mental and/or physical meltdown. When we constantly compare ourselves to others and try to "keep up," we may see God has His own plan for us—"Chill, baby!" He is not only mindful of our fragile state, but He insists on using us right where we are to carry out His will. Don't try to keep up. Just keep on. Keeping on is the best place to "be."

7

Shameless

Don't tell me not to worry, because most of the things I worry about never happen!

Source Unknown

People who suffer from generalized anxiety disorder worry about everything: relationships, their jobs, their health, their finances, whether the Braves will make it to the playoffs, etc. GAD sufferers sweat the big stuff, *and* the bigger stuff. (There's no small stuff when you have GAD.)

Always worried about the family finances, I never thought we had enough money. I bought almost my entire home's furnishings and clothes for the family from garage sales and thrift stores. I think I inherited a good portion of my frugal attitude from the most frugal person I ever met: my super-frugal mother-in-law. (I think she misplaced her genes.) When I visited her, we scavenged the neighbors' yards for treasures the night before trash day. I regularly found clothes and shoes in my size.

I subscribed to the *Tightwad Gazette*, a newsletter (no longer in circulation) for thrifty people. When the editor of the newsletter began to promote her book in the national media, she solicited letters from people interested in promoting their version of tight-waddery. The most impressive letter writers would be picked to appear with her on her mass media, cross-country book tour. So I wrote a letter about being a designer tightwad; someone who gave the impression she spent a lot of money, but in reality everything she owned and wore was cheap.

Unaware that my letter had made its way to Phil Donahue's producers, I never told Fred I wrote it. I figured the letter would be trashed in Donahue's reject pile.

One afternoon, Donahue's producers called. They liked my letter. I auditioned for my guest appearance over the phone. Fred overheard the whole thing and was quite alarmed. He knew something big was happening. Not only does Fred mistrust the media, but he has never been a fan of most TV talk shows. When he found out I'd been accepted as a guest on the show, Fred tried to convince me not to go. He said the kids needed me at home. I pointed out that I would be gone just one night and that the kids were eleven and thirteen, no longer in diapers, in case he hadn't noticed. Besides, *he* would be there.

The Donahue incident occurred during the same period when I was learning to communicate feelings like anger with my husband. I used a forceful and loud tone of voice whenever necessary to get his attention. My attitude, admittedly, was a bit too shameless: *Yo Fred! I have developed assertiveness and am no longer afraid of you! Nanny nanny, boo boo!* But in this instance I didn't raise my voice. I calmly told him I was going because I thought flying to New York and being on the show would be a thrill.

When Fred realized that he couldn't stop me, he withdrew. I admit that I wavered about my decision because he was so strongly opposed to my upcoming adventure. I thought maybe he knew something that I didn't; like, had God told him the plane was going to crash? Or worse, did he have foreknowledge that a precocious runaway booger would be clinging to the outskirts of my nasal cavity on live, national TV? Despite my paranoia about the booger man coming to get me, I made final plans to go. Fred and I both slept fitfully due to the tension between us.

I Stripped on Donahue

My part on *The Donahue Show* was a success. I brought with me several outfits purchased from thrift stores, consignment stores, and garage sales, which I packed into two huge suitcases for a one-night TV stand. However, I had no idea what I was going to do with all those clothes, and the producers of the show weren't much help.

The morning of the show, I woke up with a brilliant idea. I would strip! A one-woman fashion show was the inspired solution to showcase my cheap clothes. I engineered a way to put on four outfits all at once, rolling up pant legs underneath a skirt, which was underneath another skirt, with blazers worn over sweaters. I had extra jackets, vests, and belts on a hanger in the order I needed. As I proceeded to de-layer, or strip, I told the audience where I purchased each item and how much it cost. I was heckled at one point, but I handled it well by making the heckler look foolish. My new awareness of how to handle rejection came in handy, and hopefully was an inspiration to timid people everywhere.

The Donahue Show was so much fun and I was on such a cloud flying back to Atlanta (bad pun) that Fred in pouting mode hardly entered my mind. When he greeted me at the airport, he smiled and asked, "How'd it go?" I told him what a great time I had. When he saw the show he was *proud* of me. My son, however, was horrified. He denied it was his mother stripping on Donahue, when asked by a teacher. He still denies it, and he's twenty-nine. My daughter was ambivalent, but my parents, friends, and neighbors were quite excited.

For Fred's birthday I made him a special commemorative shirt which said, "My Wife was on the Donahue Show." When I saw him wearing it, I was so proud of him for coming out, even though he only wore the shirt when he went to the bathroom.

Fru-Gal

Happily for Fred, I did not become famous, and Hollywood agents did not ask me to audition for a low-budget remake of *Gypsy*. I did do several local television appearances, and even guested on a talk show in my hometown as a result of being on Donahue. I christened myself "Fru-Gal," and took my clothes off on every TV station in Atlanta. I did one more national show: *Rolonda*. Fred took my appearances in stride, and even represented me in true agent fashion when I was preparing for *Rolonda*.

After several guest spots, I decided that I'd had my fill of Phil, Rolonda, and gang. Each TV gig required a tremendous amount of work. I purchased and put together several outfits, and each one had to be new and different from the previous appearance. I washed and ironed everything, engineered the clothes so I stripped in the right order, and was expected to perform for free? I earned fame, but no fortune. There was no financial future in being Fru-Gal, ironically, but I *so* enjoyed my fifteen-plus minutes of fame.

I was beginning to think more clearly, probably due to spiritual growth and chemical help—as in antidepressant. And I wasn't anxious to perform just for attention's sake. I was accepting myself and no longer had to be brazen and shameless to prove I was somebody. After all, if Fred, Mr. Rogers, and God liked me just the way I was, then I should too. Feeling at peace with my new, calmer identity, I determined to wean myself from the antidepressant, as I *thought* it had done its work. (This was prior to my tipsy trip to West Palm Beach with Fred in Chapter Six.)

Our marriage grew during this pivotal time, because Fred and I were connecting. On Christmas Day of '93, I wrote him a poignantly mushy letter that ended with:

I look forward to a New Year filled with mutual honor, respect, and love.

Mutual humor was also a vital ingredient needed when we forgot to honor, respect, and love. And since we still forget a lot, we laugh a lot.

Marriages and Thunderstorms—Both Made in Heaven

Yes, I needed courage to strip on Donahue, but it took more courage to be emotionally exposed around Fred.

I'm no marriage counselor, but I've been wounded in the war between the state of matrimony and disharmony, and I feel my experiences form a critical base for what I share. It took me years to start communicating gut level feelings with Fred. But I never gave up, and the truth set us both free. I've observed many marriages with a disconnect, or a short circuit between the husband and wife. (For further reading on communication differences between the sexes, read *Men Are from Mars, Women Are from Venus,* by John Gray.)

In some marriages, the husband (lets take Fred, for example) may be a control freak, and the wife (me, for example) believes her God-given role is to please her husband at any cost. She becomes submissive for submission's sake, sacrificing her personality and character by turning into someone she's not. Wherever the wife goes, there she's *not*, and being someone she's not can cause her to be physically and mentally stressed and dysfunctional. A) And as the wife, I ought to know, because I used to be someone I was not. But now I'm not who I wasn't. I now lean towards the *fun* part of dys-fun-ctional.

I'm going to close this chapter the same way I started it: with Phil. Only this time I'll be doing my best impression of "Dr. Phil":

It's time to get real. If your wife is chronically depressed, anxious, or stressed, stop and listen to her. Her feelings are real. Don't gripe at her to get a grip. She's probably already grasped gripping. If she's headed in a downward cycle, get help: through counseling, a doctor, or both. Support her. Unconditional love promotes healing. If you either ignore or diminish the seriousness of her situation, you'll intensify and perpetuate the problem.

If your husband is chronically depressed, anxious, or stressed, stop and listen to him. He may not be in touch with his feelings, but his body is communicating pain. Sure, you don't expect your macho man to become emotionally weak, but some do. Even macho men need *mucho* unconditional love and support.

Love never fails.

A) There is usually an interplay between genetic vulnerability and stress. If genetic vulnerability to an illness such as depression is great, the person will have depression whether there is stress present or not. If the genetic vulnerability is minor, a big dose of stress may be needed to trigger an emotional illness. This model is true for many physical illnesses as well. Stress not only changes the brain chemistry, but it can also result in the death of brain cells. Fortunately, brain cells can regenerate if the stress is removed or treated.

ℋealing Words

1John 4:18 says, "There is no fear in love. But perfect love drives out fear, because fear has to do with punishment. The one who fears is not made perfect in love."

If husband and wife continue to work on perfecting their love for each other, fear of the spouse's motivation or response is not an issue.

"In your anger do not sin." Ephesians 4:26

Is this doable? Yes, but for many of us, the "have anger, don't sin" directive will take a little practice and a lot of prayer. If we can learn to deal with anger appropriately and quickly, we'll have less chance of acting out angry emotions. The key to dealing effectively with anger is to learn to direct it in ways that honor God.

8

Fred Catches the Bug

What a waste it is to lose one's mind, or not to have a mind is being very wasteful. How true that is.

Dan Quayle, misquoting the NAACP slogan:
"A Mind is a Terrible Thing to Waste."

I'd come into the bedroom, where Fred laid in bed, reading a book. He'd been both anxious and depressed all weekend but hadn't talked about it. I impulsively jumped on the bed, and with an attempt at humor said, "Does my honey have a boo-boo in his brain? Mommy rub it and make it feel all better."

With a circular motion, I very slowly massaged his forehead. Within seconds he closed his eyes, put his book down, and his whole countenance changed. A minute later with his eyes closed and appearing relaxed, he said, "I have never had such a quick reversal of mental torment. I don't know what you're doing or how you're doing it, but something is happening."

I continued the rubdown for twenty minutes and he fell asleep. Next morning I rubbed his head again for good luck; plus I was curious to know if this was a placebo effect or the real deal. As luck would have it, Fred was still one mellow fellow. The rub really worked. And so did Fred, even though just two days earlier he told me he was going to take several days off because he was mentally drained. Glad I rubbed him the right way. A)

A) Re: Fred's head rubbing. I believe Shelley's humor and head massage helped Fred change his focus. He had been absorbed in, and captured by, certain worries. Shelley's intervention brought him comfort and a change of focus from problems, to appreciation of a supportive partner and a new sense of ability to overcome problems. A 10 percent change can result in feeling 90 percent better.

Too bad I didn't know how to rub Fred the right away until a few years ago. We'll never know if regular rubdowns could have averted his emotional middle-age meltdown in the mid-'90s.

No More Mr. Tough Guy

One reason I married Fred was that he reeked of stability compared to my other boyfriends. Other guys I had dated were messed up in some way: They were dependent on me for emotional support (codependent), had ADD, or were obsessive-compulsive, depressed, alcoholic, etc. Perhaps I dated them because they made me feel better about my own flaws. After all, I wasn't as messed up as they were. Then here comes Fred, who did not *appear* to fit the above categories. But Fred had a few surprises tucked under his tough exterior.

After we married, I found out that my stable husband had once been severely and dangerously depressed over a previous divorce. In his despair, he remembered his friend Lonnie, who often talked about Jesus and being born again. He called Lonnie, who led him in the "Sinner's Prayer," and Fred was saved, *glory be to Jay-sus!*

Following this spiritual Kodak moment, Fred took a few weeks off to recover from his depression. He regrouped fairly quickly, with no professional help. His quick recovery was probably due to his youthful age of twenty-seven, his friend Lonnie's prayers, and the fact that this was his first major bout with depression. We learned from experience that each successive depressive episode usually tends to be more debilitating.

While Fred recovered emotionally, he grew spiritually and became active in a Pentecostal church. Every Sunday he found peace of mind at the altar, where he got saved at least thirty times.

"What'll I Do, What'll I Do?"

My grandmother used to laugh while telling this story about me, which she did—at least thirty times. When I was three, I got up in the middle of the night, climbed onto the kitchen counter, and knocked over a mixer and large white porcelain bowl, which crashed into a million pieces on the floor. Being three, I had a long resume of experience on how to make messes, but little background on how to resolve them. I decided on a solution of crying out: "What'll I do? What'll I do? What'll I do?" Whereupon my grandmother came downstairs, soothed me, and picked up the pieces.

One bleak February day, Fred came home needing soothing himself. Turns out he was heading in the same direction as the white porcelain mixing bowl. He was highly agitated due to job stress. He didn't sleep that night, and he was more distressed the next day. I was distressed too— "What'll I do? What'll I do? What'll I do?" was about all I could muster. And just who did he think he was? I was the one who was supposed to have emotional problems. Men were supposed to get men problems, like enlarged prostates and pulled groins. Besides the fact he was upstaging me, he was also frightening me. His downward cycle continued, and even though I was experienced at handling my own anxiety, I was clueless to help Fred. I "What'll I do-odled?" for days.

We later learned through mental health professionals that the circumstance that knocks us into an emotional frenzy is a trigger, and not usually the root cause of the problem. Many of us aren't aware of our emotional fragility until the stress is over and we find ourselves on the losing end of Mental Russian Roulette. Like, how come we handled stress OK before, and now that we're older, we're not OK with stress? According to Dr. James Mallory, psychiatrist, it has to do with the aging process. B)

Fred and I discussed possible reasons for his anxiety, and agreed he should have a physical, since physical problems like thyroid and pituitary imbalances, liver disease,[1] and even viruses[2] can create symptoms of emotional disorders. With the exception of one elevated liver enzyme, Fred's examination and lab results were normal.

A silver lining: Even though Fred didn't understand *my* problem, because of his own fragility, he developed compassion and no longer hassled me. His change *greatly* helped improve my unstable state of mind.

B) The aging process eventually leads to fewer brain cells and decreased blood supply. However, aging can also yield greater maturity and experience at overcoming, and therefore greater confidence in the future. Aging also results in loss of physical wellbeing and loss of loved ones. Problems such as these always put us at a crossroads. Either we grow in our faith and become less vulnerable to stress, or our faith weakens and we become more vulnerable.

But how could I maintain emotional, mental, and spiritual strength if Fred went down? His anxious behavior alarmed me.

He had another blood test and this time *all* his liver enzymes were elevated. He lost weight, was weak, tired, and wanted to do nothing except sit on the screened-in porch, watch the trees grow, and think negative thoughts.

When Fred wasn't listening to my somewhat forced "It's going to be OK" sunny outlook, he read and reread Barry Sears' diet book *The Zone*, and changed his eating habits to see if he would feel better. *The Zone* diet was a mixed bag; some of his liver enzyme levels temporarily lowered, but he lost weight he didn't need to lose, and he didn't feel any better.

On an ultrasound, his liver appeared borderline normal size, but stones showed up in his gallbladder. We saw several doctors, who agreed that the gallbladder needed to come out in order to eliminate possible liver irritation.

Honey I've Shrunk My Brain (?)

At the time of Fred's gallbladder diagnosis, my sleep was irregular and I was restless. I hoped the root problem might not be anxiety. I was rooting for hormones, since I was in perimenopause. I didn't want another prescription for an antidepressant. My brain should have been fixed, I thought wrongly, since I'd taken the antidepressant drug longer than what was considered normal for depressed or anxious brains. In the early to mid-'90s, antidepressants were usually prescribed for six months to a year, according to my psychiatrist. Another misunderstanding—I thought the antidepressant was like a vaccine—once you take it you're immune from the disease forever. Obviously this is not true for everyone.

Some individuals need more time and longer rounds of medication and counseling to restore brain chemistry, according to Dr. Mallory, psychiatrist. Stress hormones produced during long-term negative life experiences can cause areas of the brain to shrink. The shrinkage causes imbalances in the chemicals responsible for mental wellbeing, unless and until the brain's hard wiring can be altered.[3]

Wanting to know if stress hormones, female hormones, or both were acting up, I made an appointment with an OB-GYN. I had a hunch that perimenopause was the paramount reason for my accelerated stress. I hunched wrongly, although I'm certain the slight hormone shifts were a factor.

Dang

The doctor said my estrogen levels were fine. Dang. Estrogen deprivation sure sounded good to me; just put on a patch and you're peachy. (This was prior to the most current medical research regarding the dangers of long-term hormone use.)

I asked the doctor for a tranquilizer prescription. She refused to give me one. While attempting to appear casual and smooth on the outside, I was really nutty and chewed up on the inside. I couldn't fool her, and she recommended I see a psychiatrist. Hey! Doctors gave tranquilizers to my other women friends. What was it about me that set off their alarm? I would save time, effort, and money if I could obtain my mental health drug stash from the OB-GYN.

A related note from psychologist Dr. Melanie Wilson:

It's usually more expensive to see a psychiatrist than other medical practitioners. Insurance companies are reluctant to pay for mental health treatment, and the patient's copayment is almost always higher than it would be for a physical illness. Treating mental illness is a complicated undertaking. We know so little about the brain in comparison with the rest of the body. The treatment and results are imprecise and unpredictable, thus the costs are higher. However, if people received adequate mental health care, insurance companies would actually save money. Depression alone costs our economy billions of dollars in lost wages and production.

Wired for Worry

I immediately called the psychiatrist's office. But since I'd not seen Dr. C. for over a year, I needed an hour-long appointment. The next available one was a month away. At this point I knew what my problem was and just wanted drugs, so I decided to take my chances with a new psychiatrist.

The new doctor listened to my standard list of symptoms. I then asked him why my brain didn't unwind on its own. He said, "It's the way you're wired." I *knew* that—I wanted to hear something profound, like, "your brilliant mind is just too complex for its own good." But he wasn't impressed with my brilliant mind. In his notes, he referred to me as a "housewife with generalized anxiety disorder." He gave me a prescription for Desyrel (an antidepressant) and samples of Zoloft—a drug similar to Prozac. I told him I would try the Desyrel, which had worked so well before. This time the drug was a disaster. Within three days my nasal passages became dry as dust, so I ditched the Desyrel.

Even without the Desyrel to combat my mild depression and chronic anxiety, I managed to rally and concentrate my efforts on Fred. He was still losing weight and had gallbladder symptoms such as indigestion and nausea. We didn't know that his stomach problems were probably due to his anxiety, *not* his gallbladder. He never experienced a gallbladder attack.

Dumb and Dumber Have Great Expectations

Fred, always cold to the idea of a doctor cutting on him, suddenly warmed to the suggestion of outpatient gallbladder surgery. We were both really hopeful that the surgery would correct *all* his problems, mental and physical. We were both really stupid, too.

The day of surgery, Fred was quite calm. The doctor informed us they would do a liver biopsy during the gallbladder surgery, so the operation might take a few minutes longer. Fred was back in his room within an hour. He was not in any physical pain, but he was acting really weird. The doctor came in and said the liver was a bit red and irritated, but otherwise appeared fine, and that he removed the gallbladder with no problem. He didn't seem to think Fred's weirdness was worrisome, gave him a prescription for pain pills, and sent us home.

The next day Fred became more anxious about his anxiety. He called the surgeon and asked for a prescription for the tranquilizer Ativan. I knew they weren't going to give it to him, based upon my experience.

As I picked up his Ativan prescription, I continued to obsess over why it was so difficult for me, yet so easy for everyone else to get *that* prescription filled. I looked in the mirror to see if I had an anxiety aura, or a "deer in the headlights" affect going on.

A week went by, and Fred showed no improvement. I encouraged him to get a quick appointment with the last psychiatrist I had seen. The doctor's diagnosis was *affective mood disorder.* He thought the problem was temporary and probably related to the stress of surgery.

Fred was uplifted by the doctor's diagnosis until he thought things through. He admitted to me that, at least on a subconscious level, he believed the surgery would fix his gallbladder *and* his problems at work. He had convinced himself that the crummy way he felt severely undermined his ability to work, thus causing *all* the stress. He had wakened from the anesthesia with a jolt, realizing he had unrealistic expectations. His gallbladder was not the enemy; the enemy was his brain.

Gray Expectations

I had great compassion for Fred, and was becoming what was known as a wounded healer; someone who's been there, done that, and can therefore be of help to the person who is suffering.[4] At the time however, I felt like a fatally wounded healer. I saw no improvement in Fred. His outlook was bleak and his faith remained weak. I persevered anyway.

"Everything is turning into shades of gray," Fred said. The only tangible thing he could focus on was me. He clung to me like a life preserver, begging me to pray with him and for him. So I did, but who was going to pray for me? I needed my own life preserver, or at least "Swimmies." My Swimmies came in the way of Zoloft. I began taking the samples the psychiatrist gave me at my last appointment. Within nine days the Zoloft zapped me out of my funk.

But Fred's funk continued. He said everything was out of focus—even the kids. They were fading away into his Sea of Discontent. Thankfully, the kids weren't aware they were out to sea. Sensitive to the fact that their dad wasn't well, they still did what teenagers are supposed to do during summer vacation: swim, babysit, play with friends and computer games, and bug their moms to take them to the mall.

Since Fred had already taken off three weeks from work, he felt guilty that he wasn't back on the job. I tried to persuade him to take more sick days, but he refused. His first day back to work, he came home and started drinking—a disastrous idea.

Alcohol is a depressant, and when you're already depressed, it can be deadly. I begged Fred not to go to work the next day, and after several hours, he agreed. I made an emergency appointment with Dr. C.

It All ADDs Up

In Dr. C.'s office, Fred spewed out short, choppy blasts of disconnected thoughts and sentences. His rapid fire speech was like hitting the doctor with a machine gun full of mental diarrhea. After a few minutes Dr. C. interrupted Fred's onslaught and said, "Well, I'm not sure what your other problems are, but I know one thing—you have ADD" (attention deficit disorder).

ADD is an inability of the brain to focus and shut out internal and external distractions, resulting in scattered partial responses to many stimuli at once.[5] Fred calls ADD simply a lack of self-control.

We were not surprised at the diagnosis, as Fred had often confided in me that he had difficulty focusing. He certainly fit the profile of an ADD sufferer, as described in the book *Driven to Distraction*.[6]

The ADD diagnosis explained a lot of things, like Fred's extreme frustration when he couldn't figure out how to fix things around the house, and why he insisted on keeping a series of lists. Lists were Fred's lifelines to clarity. If I failed to keep a grocery list, he fussed and fumed. He especially hated running low on rolls—of toilet paper. Knowing we had a stash of TP in the house gave him great security and helped him think more clearly. I personally don't get that.

Related to his ADD and/or his personality, he did not like surprises, and was uncomfortable around large groups of people. He never liked more than four dinner guests, and preferred two. Parties annoyed him, and sitting in church or attending a ball game could be aggravating. Even being around me was sometimes too much for him. I personally don't get that either.

His ADD brain was incapable of filtering all the information bombarding it. Non-ADDers can shut off much of the data and ignore anything they consider irrelevant. ADDers lack that ability.[7] Fred's constant struggle to focus resulted in frustration, anxiety, irritability, and aggravation. Now I get it.

ADD was the least of Fred's problems requiring urgent treatment. His brain burn out—the anxiety and depression—were far more serious. Dr. C. prescribed Prozac, which works wonders for the majority of people, but not Fred. Within a few days he stopped taking Prozac, as he felt quite agitated.

He's a Slave to His Slavic-ness

Fred stayed agitated and depressed throughout the summer. Due to his twenty-years-plus government job, he had several weeks sick leave accumulated, but he insisted on going back to work before he was ready. I informed him he wasn't in any emotional shape to go to work, but he wouldn't listen because he was half-Slavic. Translation: His work ethic was incredibly strong, as is the work ethic of most Slavs I know. He showered, shaved, suited up, and drove his half-Slavic self downtown, dragging his less motivated half-Scandinavian self behind him.

Having been back on the job for only a few days, Fred came home expressing highly irrational negative thoughts. He paced for hours, practically making a ring around the carpet.

I considered asking Fred if he would admit himself to a psychiatric hospital before he drove us both completely nuts. Then, when a friend and I were out walking, she confirmed my sense that Fred's problems were out of my reach. Fred let me take him to the hospital the next morning.

God never promised us a calm passage, just a safe landing.

Source Unknown

Healing Words

James 5:16b tells us: "The prayer of a righteous man is powerful and effective."

When our prayers are more playful than prayerful, they can still be answered. God knows our hearts and our minds, and if they're inclined toward Him, whether we're traditional or not in our approach, that's OK with Him.

"We have different gifts, according to the grace given us . . . If it is encouraging, let him encourage . . .." Romans 12: 6a, 8a

Even when we're feeling weak and fragile ourselves, if God has given us the gift of encouragement, He will give us the grace and strength to build and lift up others.

9

Fred Goes to the Not OK Corral

It's always good to file a mental Chapter 11 and reorganize.
Carson Daly, referring to Mariah Carey's meltdown (August 8, 2001)

Showdown at the Not OK Corral

First thing in the morning I called a local psychiatric hospital. A staff member said to bring Fred in immediately. He was taken into an office where he underwent a depression test. Far as I could tell, he aced it. The admittance counselor left to confer with a staff psychiatrist, who agreed that Fred should be admitted. The admittance counselor then called the insurance company for permission to admit Fred. I sat nervously while Fred paced nervously. After about an hour the counselor came back and said he was doing his best to prove Fred's case to the insurance company, but the insurers were dubious as to whether Fred's situation warranted covering him for inpatient treatment. They weren't dubious; they just didn't want to spend the money.

I was furious! What did they want—a suicide attempt? There would very likely be one, and I wasn't just talking about Fred. I was at the end of my rope, too.

After six hours of waiting and negotiating, Fred was admitted. They took us to his cottage, which was almost empty. Most of his other cottage-mates were in a group session. However, the few patients I did see disturbed me greatly. Their mouths hung open, their eyes were glazed, and they were perpetually pacing around the room. I thought, *Uh-oh, wait till the staff finds out Fred's a pacer. He'll end up with them!* I was horrified and felt like crying, but I didn't for Fred's sake. Fred seemed oblivious to the other patients and was busy listening to the hospital aide's instructions. I kissed Fred goodbye, warned him not to do any pacing, and said I would come back that night with his things.

As soon as I got in the car I had my own emotional meltdown. *"What have I done? What's going to happen now? Please God, don't punish Fred and turn him into a zucchini just because that's what he used to call me!"* I had visions of Fred morphing into a long, skinny zucchini with big feet, pacing around the room in a vegetative state.

Telling Friends and Family About Fred's Head

I came home and took a nap. I can tell you right now that if you ever drop your spouse off at the Not OK Corral, you'll definitely need a nap when you come home, because you'll be emotionally exhausted.

Soon a friend called whom I'd not talked to in several weeks. I told her that I had just admitted Fred to a mental hospital. "Fred?" she asked. "Oh my, that's incredible!" She'd known Fred for a long time, and from her perspective he had always been a stable, calm, easygoing person. Not, not, not, but he sure had people fooled, until now.

That day was our son James' sixteenth birthday, but we didn't celebrate much. I took him and a friend to ride go-carts and then treated them to burgers. God bless my kids, they were great. I told them why Fred was admitted to the hospital, as they were both teenagers, and mature enough to know the truth. They also handled Fred's long recovery process without any noticeable ill effects.

That same day I phoned Fred's boss to tell him about Fred's hospitalization. I'm not sure he understood me, because I was sobbing and incoherent. If he heard the words "psychiatric hospital," he may have been confused as to who the patient was: Fred or me.

Inpatients and Impatience

I gathered up Fred's belongings and went back to the hospital for the visiting hours. I was pleasantly surprised to see Fred smiling and carrying on a discussion with some people who looked normal. Fred introduced me to his cottage-mates, and I found them to be very pleasant and intelligent conversationalists.

Fred's spirits seemed greatly improved. I saw a transformation from a couple of hours earlier. We sat alone and he told me stories about his roommates.

"I'm rooming with a guy who's on physical disability from his job. His wife left him and he couldn't handle it. Then there's 'Sue,' who's bipolar and her medication isn't working. 'Joann' is a nineteen-year-old college student who ran out of her Prozac and didn't bother refilling the prescription. She freaked without the Prozac. 'John' is delusional. He's very nice, but thinks he works for the CIA and the FBI. They remind him not to talk about his undercover work in group therapy. The man playing the piano is a doctor. He had a falling out with his father, which triggered his breakdown. He drove here and admitted himself. That young emaciated-looking woman is into self-mutilation. The other woman is a single working mother and having problems with her teenage daughter. The mom overdosed on the combination of Prozac and alcohol. And you know, after looking at these people, I've concluded I'm not so bad off!"

I asked Fred about the perpetual pacers; he maintained that they were in the minority. Those poor souls were barely functioning and were not expected to participate with the group.

On one visit I saw a patient wearing a metal contraption around his head. It looked like someone had been playing with an erector set and was operating the guy by remote control. I had never seen this type of heavy metal therapy before and was mesmerized.

Fred pointed out the "pit," where patients under suspicion of suicide attempts slept—or didn't sleep—in full view of the nurse's station under bright lights, in a sunken area filled with couches and easy chairs.

The staff had taken Fred's Ativan away, so I slipped him one. He hid the pill in his shorts pocket. When he put his shorts back on the next morning, the pill was gone. Apparently the staff pilfered all pills while the patients slept.

The next day Fred met with Dr. H, a new psychiatrist who assessed Fred's meds and within a week would prescribe Tofranil—the drug that became the "kiss of life" for Fred.

Fred had been off the Prozac for a week and Dr. C. had switched him to Zoloft. Fred had felt disconnected on Zoloft. He also lost his appetite. Fortunately Fred's prescription didn't go to waste. As a new Zoloft-er, I welcomed the extra med.

Prozac and Zoloft are in an antidepressant group known as SSRIs: selective serotonin reuptake inhibitors. A) They worked OK for me (except for the stomach cramps with Prozac), but Fred had a different brain. Unfortunately, we couldn't pry the lid off Fred's brain and tell him he was a quart low in whatever, and he needed drug X as opposed to drug Y. Perhaps someday. B)

After four days of group therapy and daily visits with Dr. H., Fred wanted to be discharged, especially since his new roommate was a bed-wetter. He convinced Dr. H. that he was recovering, and the doctor prescribed a week of outpatient treatment.

Hope, Hope, Hopeless?

Fred felt a huge sense of accomplishment and control. He'd talked the doctor into discharging him a day early. He wrote in his journal: *I feel pretty good . . . why? Because I'm only concerned about the day! One day! I convinced the doctor to let me go—I controlled it! Work is not an issue, I've cut my losses, I'm in control. I know I can put off worry and focus till tomorrow. I have hope, hope, hope, hope, hope, hope, hope.* However, I hadn't read his journal, and I wasn't so hope, hope, hopeful that coercing the doctor into an early discharge was the right thing to do. I didn't know if Fred was recovering, or still in a crisis mode. Time would tell.

A) Antidepressants are usually classified according to which neurotransmitters they affect and how they affect them. The Prozac family includes Zoloft, Paxil, Luvox, Lexepro, and Celexa. They all increase serotonin and are called serotonin reuptake inhibitors. Effexor is called a dual reuptake inhibitor because it increases serotonin and norepinephrine. Wellbutrin is unique because it increases norepinephine and dopamine without affecting serotonin. Remeron is in a class by itself; it increases serotonin and norepinephrine. The older antidepressants like Tofranil are known as tricyclics because of their chemical structure. They increase the number of all neurotransmitters, but they also impact many other systems and thus have more side effects than the newer antidepressants. The oldest antidepressants, known as monoamine oxidase inhibitors, increase norepinephrine, serotonin, and dopamine. These are powerful antidepressants with potential side effects if one eats the wrong food or takes the wrong medicine.

B) No one knows why some people respond in a dramatic and positive way to a particular antidepressant, yet someone else gets nothing but adverse side effects from the same medication. This is true even of antidepressants in the same class.

Fred's metabolism was revved up by his high anxiety. That meant he wouldn't regain the twenty-five pounds he lost until his anxiety diminished.

We're all so different. In my entire life, I'd only lost four pounds at the most during an anxiety attack. Fred could lose four pounds in four hours.

During the next several days, whenever Fred's anxiety reached crescendo levels, at least once or twice a day, we prayed for God to calm him down. If Fred's brain stayed wired, he took a tranquilizer.

Fred and I talked nonstop during those first months of recovery. I asked him to list his most troublesome obsessive thoughts, and here's what he wrote: *Tired, unfocused, overwhelmed, feeling of foreboding, feeling very strongly I'm not supposed to work . . . except at a very low level. I want everything done, finished, so I don't have to think about it.*

Group Therapy/Hug Therapy

The hospital outpatient treatment consisted mainly of group discussions. The participants learned about everything from worry-stopping techniques to cognitive therapy. According to the book *Feeling Good*, cognitive therapy is based on the premise that negative thoughts and self-criticism often distort reality. Proponents believe that our thoughts govern our minds. Therefore we can change our feelings by stopping negative thoughts before experiencing the emotions that stem from them.[1] Fred was never able to apply the cognitive therapy concepts effectively. But the book was a bestseller, so many must be benefiting.

Fred tried a worry-stopping technique from his homework. He set aside fifteen minutes a day to worry. He chose from 3:00 p.m. to 3:15 p.m. Even though restricted to fifteen minutes a day, he'd start the next day's homework within forty-five minutes, worrying promptly from 4:00 p.m. to 4:15 p.m. Then he'd go for extra credit and start worrying again at 5:00 p.m.

Word reached various church members that Fred was in severe depressive mode. Several people were praying for his recovery. Fred had not given up on prayer, but he did wonder why God wasn't seeing the urgency of the situation. He maintained that lengthy suffering was pointless and served no purpose. I did not argue—I just held him.

Throwing Brain Darts

Prescribing medication for mental illnesses is like "throwing a dart at a target," according to Dr. C. "We never know whether we'll hit the target. That's why we often have to try different drugs." We sure knew that from Fred's experience. Even more frustrating, often two to four weeks pass before the drug starts working in the brain. It's not like getting a shot of penicillin, where the effect is almost immediate.

"For reasons rather complicated, cumulative levels of an antidepressant are needed to alter brain chemistry," added Dr. C. So, after the first try of a failed drug, the patient tries drug number two, which may not work either. Meanwhile, six weeks may have passed, with the patient becoming more miserable, despondent, and possibly suicidal. A patient may try several drugs before finding one that works. C)

Whole Lotta Shakin'

I compared Fred's mental crisis to an earthquake. The quake was over, but then came the aftershocks or *aftershakes* as I call them: mild to moderate depression and anxiety episodes. There would be a whole lot of shakin' goin' on over the next several years—in fact, things have never really stopped shakin.' That's just life, and it's OK.

C) There are some important considerations when a person is said to be non-responsive to psychiatric medications. The most common reason is that that the person is taking an inadequate dosage, or has not been on medication long enough for it to have an effect. Some antidepressants can take six-eight weeks for maximal effect. Other important reasons for patients not responding: The person needs to be on a different medication, or may need to be on a combination of antidepressants. Non-responders are often treated under the wrong diagnosis. For example, many people with depression are highly anxious and if they're on a tranquilizer, their depression will worsen. Alcohol or drug abuse will also undermine the treatment response. Some patients and even physicians are resistant to the idea of a person being on a number of different antidepressants. However, it should be noted that people who are treated for high blood pressure or heart disease are often on three or more medications for the same condition. This is also true of diabetics. Some people fail to respond to medication because non-medical factors such as spiritual, relational, vocational, or psychological are not being addressed. Some people respond better to non-traditional forms of therapy. There are many claims about nonprescription medicines that are supposed to help depression. Two that have documented research behind them are SAM-e, and 1000 mg. of EPA, an Omega-3 fatty acid.

Healing Words

"Consider it pure joy, my brothers, whenever you face trials of many kinds, because you know that the testing of your faith develops perseverance. Perseverance must finish its work so that you may be mature and complete, not lacking anything."

James 1:2-4

God perseveres right along with us. He often does his biggest work in us over time, giving insight, understanding, and maybe a total transformation. A speedy deliverance might not guarantee the results needed for permanent change.

Romans 5:3-5a says that we are to "rejoice in our sufferings, because we know that suffering produces perseverance; perseverance, character; and character, hope. And hope does not disappoint us . . ."

We may have a hard time rejoicing in the midst of our suffering, but we can trust that God is with us, wanting to do a work in us, even in the midst of our negative emotional state. May we all have hope eternal to help carry us through the trials of life.

Fred's Worry-Stopping List

1. Set aside the same time of day to worry. Concentrate on worrying only during that time.
2. Ask yourself the question: "What is the absolute worst thing that can happen"?
3. Talk yourself through your worries, using the techniques you've learned. Just STOP!
4. Rather than worrying about the negative things that might happen, imagine what you most want to have happen. Then develop a plan to begin to move toward that goal.
5. Understand that worrying robs your time and produces stress.
6. Compile a worry list. Include all the things you find yourself worrying about. Make a separate list for worries you can do something about, and those you can't do anything about. For those you can do something about, write down an action you can take to combat the worry.
7. Take action. Many of the things we worry about can be dealt with by having an effective plan in place. Set and define goals, identify actions that can be taken to accomplish your goals.
8. Analyze your goals. If you're not acting on them, you may need to rethink your goals or delete them from your list.
9. Get rid of the guilt for not worrying—worrying simply is a waste of your time and life.

10

Drugs-R-Us

If you can't make it better, you can laugh at it.

Erma Bombeck

It was one in the morning, less than twenty-four hours after Fred had been discharged from the hospital. I awoke to a very agitated Fred talking loudly on the phone to Dr. H. "I'm hallucinating and feeling disconnected. Am I having a drug interaction problem? I'm seeing talking dogs and feeling spacey."

Fred hung up, telling me he had scheduled an emergency appointment with the doctor the next day. Confused and frightened, he paced the rest of the night, trying to shut up the talking dogs. Anyone who has hallucinated will tell you the experience is terrifying; anyone except psychotics, who may not be aware they're hallucinating. A)

During the appointment, the doctor expressed concern that Fred was becoming psychotic. I told the doctor I wasn't sure about that, but I did tell him I thought Fred's obsessive thought patterns were . . . well . . . obsessive. The doctor added obsessive-compulsive disorder to Fred's list of diagnoses. This new diagnosis meant a new drug prescription. Fred wouldn't hear of more drugs. Instead, he asked the doctor if a drug interaction could have caused the hallucinations. Dr. H. said that was highly unlikely, but our pharmacist thought it was indeed possible for the Zoloft/Klonopin combination to cause hallucinations in susceptible individuals.

A) Drugs that induce hallucinations cause the brain to transmit an impulse inappropriately to a receiving center in the brain. If the impulse goes to the back part of the brain, one will have a visual hallucination. If it goes to the lateral part of the brain, one will have an auditory hallucination. If it goes to some of the central parts of the brain, a person may have a transient wonderful feeling, or feel terrified or depressed. These experiences are somewhat like having a dream or a nightmare, only the person is awake.

Finally, a breakthrough. At the next office visit, Dr. H. prescribed Tofranil. This old antidepressant that had been around since the '50s was key to lifting Fred's depression.

Obsessions

After three days Fred wanted to quit the Tofranil, even though he hadn't developed side effects. He didn't feel better and was frustrated and impatient. The greatest challenge in treating Fred over the years was to keep him on his medication.

Within a few more days, Fred noticed a difference in his mood. He felt longer moments of calm, and I noticed minor improvements. Two of Fred's distractions during his recovery were playing Scrabble with me, and obsessing about his high pulse rate—a common side effect of his med. Fred couldn't sense his heart beating faster, but one day he took his resting pulse. It was in the nineties, and a cause for unrest. So he took his pulse about every ten minutes while awake, and a few times at night as well.

He obsessed about his physical health in general. Anything that was slightly off-kilter caused him great distress, such as bulging veins in his legs. I told him the veins bulged because he'd lost so much weight in his legs, but he didn't buy it. Fred thought he had irreversible varicose veins. He had never been vain about his veins before.

Flashback

One Saturday morning we heard what sounded like a helicopter buzzing the trees over our house. Sure enough, there it was, hovering over our cul de sac at a dangerously low level. Fred watched it for a moment, and assessed the situation as "code red." He yelled for the kids and me to run for cover. We went in the basement for a minute, but I was curious, so I came back upstairs. Fred grabbed his gun and ran out the front door yelling, "Heads up, I'm locked and loaded!" *Locked and loaded?* I soon realized that was gun talk for: "I'm gonna shoot you if you don't get your helicopter out of my air space!" (Little did we know it was our nice, thrill-seeking neighbor copping some "fun" in the 'copter.)

As my concern rose, so did the helicopter. It flew over a nearby cul de sac, hovering for a minute before it took off for good. What a relief—I avoided having to explain to the police why a bullet-riddled helicopter was in our front yard filled with bloody, screaming people.

On a more serious note, I think Fred overreacted to situations due to mental fragility triggered by job stress. Combine that with untreated ADD, anxiety, and depression, and you've cooked up a recipe for fuzzy thinking.

Fred's Up and Down Recovery—He's "Yo Yo Pa"

Fred continued to make slow but steady improvement. We made regular visits to Dr. H.'s office, where Fred gave a negative and dismal mood report. I counter-balanced with a more positive, realistic account, citing strides I'd noticed. I accompanied Fred to his appointments because every patient, *especially* a mental health patient, should have an advocate. Doctors need rational observations on the patient's progress, and patients aren't often rational or aware enough to know how they're doing.

After several more weeks, Fred was well enough to return to work. Fred's co-workers were aware of his difficulties and treated him like the fragile fellow he was. An added bonus: his medication was not only an effective antidepressant, but also helped his ADD. B) Once Fred stabilized, our life returned to normal. In fact, life was better than normal; it was exquisite. I had never seen Fred so mellow. Stuff that normally bothered him, didn't. As Fred started to feel OK, so did I.

By the following January Fred had been on Tofranil for four-plus months and thought that was enough time for the med to do its work, but Dr. H. had told Fred he might need medication for one to two years. Fred was Fred however, and in charge of his own head. I tried to talk him out of stopping the medication, but he told me he was just fine. Besides, he was tired of the racing pulse and leg tremor side effects.

Going off the drug was a big mistake. Fred was OK for a couple of

---

B) There are primarily three classes of medications that have helped ADD: certain antidepressants, stimulants, and the new alerting medications (that are not actually stimulants) show some promise. They all work by helping the brain to ignore unimportant stimuli and stay better focused on the more important issue at hand. ADD is genetic, not acquired. The primary deficit seems to be that the "brain filter" lets too much data sift through to consciousness, so that the person has chronic message or sensory overload.

months until he began a new job assignment. The position started with a three-week training session in Austin, Texas. Uh-oh—change in routine. Fred's brain liked routine. Fred's brain did not like change. Bad brain.

He left for Austin on a Sunday morning and seemed OK, although he did inform me he hadn't slept all night. He blamed his insomnia on a few glasses of wine he'd had at a dinner party the prior evening. Sunday night I received a phone call from a panic-stricken Fred, 150 miles from Austin. His head was cycling with negative thoughts. I talked and prayed with him, and he calmed down for the rest of the ride.

When he flew home for the weekend at the two-week class interval, his mental state appeared stable. But when he arrived home at the end of the training session, I recognized the signs of impending doom and gloom. This time I firmly lectured him: "You are not going to work tomorrow. You should never have gone off the medication. I am not going through this again and neither are you!"

My tough love tactics paid off, and this time we made an appointment with Dr. C., our all-time favorite psychiatrist. Fred did not want to go back on the Tofranil. He had been reading more about Prozac, and decided to give it a second chance. He stayed on Prozac for four weeks, but his improvement was inconsistent. He read more about various antidepressants, went back to Dr. C. and told him that he wanted to try Serzone, a fairly new antidepressant. Fred had more success with Serzone, but it didn't help his ADD symptoms.

Note: In 2004 Serzone was taken off the market. It was found to cause liver damage and liver failure in some patients. Had we known this information in '96, Fred would not have requested the medication, due to his own sensitive liver.

Fred eventually tried Ritalin for his ADD. It worked wonders, but he became very irritable when coming down from the medication. Doctors refer to this as "rebounding." C) I did not want to be in the same zip code as Fred when he was rebounding from Ritalin.

During this relapse, we decided to seek another psychiatrist's opinion. To show you how subjective psychiatry can be, the second doctor labeled Fred's major problem as obsessive-compulsive disorder. The doctor completely shrugged off ADD as a diagnosis.

C) Rebound is a phenomenon that comes from a stimulant when it is rapidly metabolized, causing the person to feel washed out. The longer-acting ADD medications and new alerting medications such as time-release Adderal and Straterra are less likely to cause rebound.

At our next visit to Dr. C., we told him the diagnosis made by the other psychiatrist. Dr. C. disagreed. He said Fred had obsessive personality *traits*, but not obsessive-compulsive *disorder*. I'd come to the same conclusion. Fred displayed too few symptoms. Anyone who uses the same towel five days in a row after showering is *not* obsessive-compulsive.

Fred did OK while on Serzone, but not great. He read a considerable amount on ADD and experimented with self-medication. He tried Gingko Biloba, an herb that supposedly stimulates the brain; Kava Kava, a root with a calming effect; and even nicotine. Fred said he could think more clearly for about fifteen minutes after he smoked one of his two daily cigarettes. His greatest find was caffeine pills. He said caffeine worked better than Ritalin or anything else he had tried for the ADD.

Staying Alive From Nine to Five

Even with the dietary, herb and vitamin, caffeine and nicotine enhancements, Fred had trouble focusing on and managing his job duties. He lacked the mental energy to accomplish the simplest task, with or without Ritalin or caffeine pills.

Finally, we experienced a breakthrough. A new government policy allowed several employees—including Fred—to work on cases from home. Fred's stress level lowered. He still woke up feeling anxious, but a caffeine pill quelled the negative feelings and helped him focus.

It's OK to Be Chemically Challenged

Even though Fred's constant negative self-talk surely tried his two best buddies' patience, they were always there for him. These men knew the meaning of unconditional love. One guy fondly referred to Fred as his chemically-challenged friend.

We had passed the year mark since Fred's discharge from the psychiatric hospital, and several months since his relapse had elapsed. I felt he continued to suffer from mild depression and mild obsessive thoughts along with the ADD, but at least we weren't in a crisis situation. Fred's favorite quote around that time was, "The mass of men live lives of quiet desperation" (Henry David Thoreau). I tell you, that Fred was such a clown.

Fred spent every spare minute educating himself about his mind and brain. He bought heavy-duty books such as the *DSM-III*, a doctor's reference guide to mental illnesses (American Psychiatric Association), the best-selling *Emotional Intelligence* by Daniel Goleman (Bantam Books), *The Emotional Brain* by Joseph Ledoux (Touchstone), and *The Feeling of What Happens* by Antonio Damasio (Harvest Books).

An excellent article on male depression noted that the numbers of depressed men were rising, not only because more men were getting help, but also because men were suffering in greater numbers. The author reported that depression was triggered by confusion in an increasingly technological world, and he expounded on the biological roots of depression—i.e., imbalanced brain chemistry and genetic factors.[1]

Several current self-help books focus on men and depression. One, *I Don't Want to Talk About It* by Terrance Real (Scribner), states that depression is a hidden epidemic among men; that males, taught to disavow their feelings, turn to drinking or drugs. Fortunately, more and more men are seeking treatment;[2] a point worth emphasizing.

Fred and I saw the humor in our joint predicaments—his depression, my anxiety. We joked about starting a Hussey's House of Hot Drugs chain. At one time we had all these prescribed medications in our cabinet: Serzone, Wellbutrin, Klonopin, Risperdal, Imipramine, Trazadone, Prozac, Zoloft, Buspar, Ativan, Ambien, Anafranil, Ritalin, and Cylert.

Uh-oh. I feel a song coming on. There's no reason for this song, but there is rhyme. This is medicated to the one I love:

"My Favorite Pills"

Ritalin, Cylert: They help with brain fog,
With Ativan, Ambien, we sleep like a log,
Trazadone, Klonopin, Anafranil,
We feel better just taking a pill!

When depression bites,
When anxiety stings,
When we're feeling sad,
We just pop a Prozac or Zoloft or Buspar,
And then we don't feel . . . so bad!

To lower our reliance on medication and reduce stress, Fred and I exercised regularly. Fred usually ran in place, and I ran my mouth while walking with a friend, or played tennis, or worked out with aerobic tapes.

Left Behind

I also read copiously but, unlike Fred, I read books with a spiritual and psychological emphasis that addressed my particular (peculiar?) issues. Occasionally, I found an article or a book with a scientific slant that caught my attention. Since I was a southpaw, I was intrigued by Stanley Coren's *The Left-Hander Syndrome*. The author said left-handed people were more prone to anxiety and less emotionally stable than their right-handed brothers and sisters.[3]

Artistic Angst

Artist Vincent Van Gogh wasn't left handed, but he was anxious. Van Gogh was once hospitalized with a mental disorder. He said, "It is only too true that a lot of artists are mentally ill—it's a life which, to put it mildly, makes one an outsider. I'm all right when I completely immerse myself in work, but I'll always remain half crazy."[4]

My artist friend Karen says she's ninety-nine percent certain that Van Gogh was bipolar. Most of us are familiar with the story about Van Gogh cutting off his ear in a fit of madness. Self-mutilation was his self-medication. No brain drugs were available to ease his pain. His anguished mind produced paintings that are today worth millions. If he'd kept both ears and had no angst, would he have been such an awesome artist? We'll never know about Van Gogh.

If the prevailing consensus is correct, that creativity does indeed stem from the artist's right brain, does that indicate that certain aspects of mental illness are right brain rooted? Inquiring right brain minds want to know, but as of yet, science has no definitive answer.

Healing Words

"An anxious heart weighs a man down, but a kind word cheers him up." Proverbs 12:25

When we're overwhelmed with anxiety and fear, God often sends angels in the form of friends who, even though untrained as counselors, may provide stronger therapeutic support due to the bond of unconditional love.

"The heart of the discerning acquires knowledge; the ears of the wise seek it out." Proverbs 18:15

Educating ourselves about our emotional challenges can help remove some of the fear, uncertainty, and misconceptions. Education + Faith = Powerful Tools for Healthy Living.

11

Stressed for Success

It has become appallingly obvious that our technology has exceeded our humanity.

Albert Einstein

When I first went online in the late '90s, I became so enamored with the Internet that I subscribed to every e-publication and e-group offered: joke lists, business support groups, writers groups, anxious people support group, depressed people support group, spouses of depressed people support group, inspirational newsletters and devotions, small business owners networking groups, fibroid tumors support group, and menopause support group. Overwhelmed with all the support, I unsubscribed from ninety-nine percent of these.

Larry Rosen and Michelle Weil, authors of *TechnoStress* (John Wiley & Sons), say the real problem with the Internet is that we're not taught to be data-sifters. Bombarded with information, sufferers don't have enough time to handle the onslaught. We become frustrated and "technostressed." When overloaded with data, we often have trouble sleeping because our brains are so "full." The authors say one solution to technostress is to establish a time limit when searching the Web. Also, don't log on to the Internet or use email immediately before bedtime.

It's Christmas and I'm Not Wrapped Too Tight

Back in the pre-email '70s, I was a copywriter/announcer for a small radio station in northeast Ohio. Great experience—I learned to do just about every job at that station. Unfortunately, learning and doing everything made the work and stress unrelenting. Also, I had major sugar cravings and consumed three to six donuts every morning while downing two cups of black coffee.

One Christmas Eve at the station, I wrote and produced about twenty-five radio commercials. Many had to be on the air Christmas day. I was totally strung-out and exhausted, and hadn't begun my Christmas shopping.

I finished work and my boyfriend picked me up at 4:30 p.m. We rushed to the mall and bought all my family gifts in one hour, finishing just before the mall closed, then stopped at a Chinese restaurant for dinner. As the waitress took our order, I stared blankly at the menu and burst into tears. My boyfriend excused my behavior with, "She always gets sentimental around the holidays."

I left the table, heart pounding, nerves fraying. In the ladies room I literally climbed the wall of a stall and started to bawl. Luckily, nobody was in the other stall—she would have been shocked to hear wailing noises and see hands clawing the edge. I don't know why I tried to climb *over* the edge. I was already there.

At the time, I was only twenty-four, yet had burned out. I didn't want to think, didn't want to work. Burning out at such a young age suggested that the radio business was not for me. Or perhaps Christmas was not for me. Or both.

Common sense tells me that job burnout likely occurs when you're not a good match for your work. My husband knows this. He burned out at age forty-seven after working twenty years as a CPA. Fred says he should have been a forest ranger.

Most of my stress occurred around the holiday season, in the late '80s and early to mid-'90s. My business created custom-designed holiday cards for companies. Most of my clients thought about beginning the card process in October or November. In my business, this time frame is akin to starting your Christmas shopping on Christmas Eve. Late starts left me little time to oversee all the details. I was the project coordinator for each account, loving the whole process until just before Christmas—that time of year when just about everyone loses their joy.

I allowed one of my vendors to aggravate the situation. He didn't believe in production schedules, and catered instead to customers who squeaked the loudest. Unfortunately, the only squeaking I ever did was during raucous fits of laughter. So at night I'd lie awake rehearsing explanations to clients about why their jobs were late. I suffered tension headaches daily, all because I'd never learned to assert myself.

Please Step on Me—I'm a Doormat

Another term for my "Please Step on Me—I'm a Doormat" behavior is "learned helplessness."[1] I felt helpless to change my situation. I didn't consider the possibility of using other vendors. I can now understand why people stay in dead-end jobs, why women stay in abusive relationships, etc. The brain becomes "paralyzed;" confined to a cerebral wheelchair that's stuck in a rut. And the rut has become comfortably uncomfortable.

In '92, after my therapy sessions, I had my own revelation experience on this learned helplessness issue. I faced my feelings, raised my standards, and discovered there is more than one solution to a problem— what a shocker.

Don't Mess With Stress

But I still succumb easily to problems that appear outside my control. Dr. C. told me, "Anytime you perceive a stress, your brain will react more sensitively than a 'normal' person's, because that's the way you're wired." I short-circuit more easily.

For several years I've set a goal: Prevent the stress. Right. Then after I prevent the stress, I go rid the world of terrorism.

Preventing stress only works some of the time. I can't control what happens. Dang. Family members and friends die. Accidents happen. Illness strikes. My favorite baseball team doesn't make it to the World Series. People—and my baseball team—don't cooperate with my plans. Turns out I'm never *really* in control. The whole thing is an illusion.

Stress, however, is more than an illusion. It causes mental and physical symptoms: memory loss and depression, upset stomach, fatigue, and frequent headaches. Long-term stress contributes to heart disease and high blood pressure, memory loss, and depression.[2] I have my own unique stress symptoms, and also experience *sympathy* stress pains when I'm around someone I care about who's extremely stressed. I literally feel their pain in a vulnerable area of my body—my left hip, which tends to over-produce the stress hormone cortisol,[3] causing the pain. Once, after confronting a visiting friend's mental crisis, I began limping and hobbling from one room to the next, but my friend was so stressed she never noticed. (Stressed people can be quite self-centered, so don't go looking for sympathy from them.)

Stress = Too Few Resources, Too Many Demands

And what about workaholics? For what are they killing themselves? What makes them addicted to work? I've asked a good workaholic friend of mine those questions, but she's too busy to answer. "A work addict can also be a rushaholic, careaholic and busyaholic—any person who is driven to do too much," says Diane Fassel in her book, *Working Ourselves to Death* (Backinprint.com).

The workaholics I know are driven by internal clocks of thirty-six hour days. I always thought they achieved an adrenaline rush by accomplishing stuff. Psychiatrist Dr. Mallory explained it this way: "Accomplishments may give a powerful sense of 'OK-ness.' But they don't necessarily result in an adrenaline rush. However, some of the traits that produce a workaholic often include a need for such a 'charge.' Workaholics may consciously or unconsciously place themselves in situations to promote an adrenaline rush, such as: performing complicated tasks with extreme time pressures, being overscheduled, waiting until the last minute to do something or go somewhere, driving too fast, provoking conflict, or engaging in other dangerous behavior."

When at the height of her workaholic frenzy, Jane, my Type A person-ality friend, was the mother of two teens and a preteen, working as a realtor out of her home. Jane (not her real name or occupation) is a classic workaholic, often putting in twelve-to-fourteen-hour days. For her fortieth birthday, I helped her husband plan a surprise party. I came up with the perfect invitation. The theme was the popular movie *Twister*, since Jane herself was a human tornado. The invitation depicted her head on top of a twister while her family ran for cover. Jane's husband and I reluctantly decided we'd better tell her about the party plans, in case her busy schedule conflicted. Well, Jane had us cancel the party. She was too busy to turn forty. And ten years later she was too busy for fifty. Her age has definitely not caught up with her.

Jane's stress symptoms are tightness in her chest and shortness of breath. She's realizes she is the perfect candidate for a heart attack. I asked her, "Is all this worth it?" She said "Yes—I love seeing my customers happy." Update: Jane is alive, but has slowed down a bit, from a tornado to a high wind.

Sleep researchers say that Americans like Jane are some of the most sleep-deprived people on earth. The National Sleep Foundation states that "sleep deprivation costs Americans more than $100 billion a year in lost productivity, traffic accidents, medical expenses and on-the-job injuries."[4]

"Workers who are chronically stressed on the job can expect to pay higher prices to get mental health treatment which, of course, will produce additional stress," said Steven Daviss, M.D., who responded to some questions I posed to him during an online depression chat. He added that most insurance companies cover mental illnesses at the "psychiatric reduction" rate. "If depression, for instance, is caused by a physical condition like hypothyroidism, the insurance company will pay benefits at 80 percent. However, if a 'psychiatric code' is applied to the diagnosis, a 'brain tax' is added, and the benefits are 50 percent."

Not surprisingly, many employers have misconceptions about depression. They will hire a person with a physical disorder such as chronic asthma before they'll hire someone who has recovered from a mental illness.[5] Even though no evidence shows that the asthmatic performs better than the recovered Not OK person, apparently a stigma attaches to depression or anxiety in one's health history.[6]

Thankfully, I'm my own employer of my one person company. So I'm cutting edge on understanding this stuff, and attach no such stigma to my employee's health history.

I, the employee, thank me, the employer, for her understanding.

You're welcome.

Laugh More, Obsess About Stress Less

The book *301 Ways to Have Fun at Work* gives compelling reasons for humor in the marketplace. Laughter releases tension and increases the employee's ability to cope with stress. Some firms are finding that fun and humor in the workplace help make their employees more productive, flexible, creative, and innovative under pressure.[7]

People with obsessive-compulsive traits, like my husband, are the most likely to suffer from job stress, according to Drs. Minirth and Meier. They'll ruminate over the tiniest mistake or mildest form of criticism. Their perfectionist nature accompanies their obsessive behavior.[8] Not only was husband Fred an obsessive type, but his situation was exacerbated by ADD. Such people don't feel worthy unless they're *doing* something. Fred always said, "If a man doesn't work, he shouldn't eat." However, Fred is now retired, and I notice he's still eating.

Fred's job stress was barely manageable, even while working at home. He was "putting in the time or going through the motions," he said. He took "mental health" days or vacation whenever he could. Some mornings he would start the work day only to become frazzled by 9 a.m. I encouraged him to take the rest of the day off. He related to the following quote by Robert Frost: "The brain is a wonderful organ. It starts the moment you get up in the morning and doesn't stop until you get to the office." Fred eventually quit feeling guilty and accepted the fact that he couldn't keep up with the job the way he once did. He's always said he "burned out" at age forty-seven and felt like he had an eighty-five-year-old's brain—a comment that my eighty-seven-year-old-still-sharp father could not relate to. Fred also described the way he felt as "low mental energy."

Stress—Take It Personally

Our responses to stress are personal. Personally, my stress symptoms begin with a bad case of the cooties. Nose fondling, twitching, or face typing is a dead giveaway that I'm unraveling.

I have a teacher friend I'll call Jan who, by May of every year has suicidal thoughts. Jan is a gifted teacher, whose kids love her until she burns out—around February of every year—when her tone becomes sharp and sarcastic and she no longer has patience to deal with the students' unruly behavior. She hates her Dr. Jekyll and Mr. Hyde routine, but says she can't help it. Her teaching lacks creativity because discipline takes so much effort.

By spring, Jan's emotional arsenal contains anger, frustration, and sarcasm. Worse, she suffers low self-esteem and compares herself to every other teacher who, she is convinced, have perfect classrooms. The smallest crisis could topple her, and sometimes it does. When she's toppled, she retreats to her bedroom every day after work, not wanting any human interaction, instead watching hours and hours of TV.

Even the financially secure suffer from stress, perhaps in disproportional larger numbers. Hollywood starlets with virtually no talent and major league athletes with mucho talent can succumb. Celebrities have huge pressures to perform. The stress cycle can be vicious and seemingly endless. But if the celebrity has a good press agent, that can help.

Executive Energizer Bunnies/Dust Bunnies

My youngest brother Matt is an entrepreneur and community figure who can juggle fifteen balls at once and stay calm, without exhibiting stress symptoms. In other words: *he does not fondle or twitch his nose.* His wife Shirley, just as much a multi-tasker, does not self-fondle or twitch either. Matt and Shirley are co-owners of a successful restaurant, have three teenagers, and participate in all the kids' activities. Matt and his wife probably run on batteries, although I saw Matt naked as a baby and noticed no battery compartment. I've never seen Shirley naked.

Other, more well known "energizer bunnies" I've never seen naked include Presidents Bill Clinton and George Bush. These two are perfect examples of people who successfully compartmentalized outside stresses, even while taking on the world's problems. President Clinton, in spite of all the distractions and scandals during his terms, not only enjoyed a high job approval rating, but I give him high marks for stress tolerance as well. Fred says Bill Clinton doesn't suffer much stress because he has healthy amygdalae; the part of the brain where fear and negative emotion reside. A) It's probably more complicated than that, but Fred's big on

A) The amygdala is a crucial structure of the limbic system, which also includes the hypothalamus. This system is largely responsible for feelings that accompany or induce actions. Example: A person hears an ominous sound in the dark. The cortex sends a signal to the amygdala, which sends feelings of fear back to the cortex, which then sends a signal to the hypothalamus, which ends up producing adrenaline and other stress substances. The amygdala is probably involved in all strong feeling states.

giving simple answers to complex problems. And President Bush, in spite of the 9/11 crisis, the unpopular war in Iraq, and his consistently low approval ratings in the public opinion polls, remained unflappable, calm, and resolute throughout his terms—"staying the course."

Then there's Fred and me: more like dust bunnies than energizer bunnies. Neither Fred nor I will ever run for president. Our amygdalae would hold us back. But we've learned to accept who we are. And for the record, we *can* feel your pain.

Healing Words

"Buy the truth and do not sell it; get wisdom, discipline and understanding." Proverbs 23:23

Before any positive change occurs in our thinking and behavior on an issue, we first have to confront the truth about our feelings. Confronting the truth can be the most difficult part of the battle because we've conditioned our minds to believe "lies" for so long. May you have a "revelation experience" in your own life, setting you free and leading to wisdom, discipline, and understanding.

"Come to me, all you who are weary and burdened, and I will give you rest. Take my yoke upon you and learn from me, for I am gentle and humble in heart, and you will find rest for your souls. For my yoke is easy and my burden is light." Matthew 11:28-30

Sleep and rest are so important to our mental, emotional, physical, and spiritual wellbeing. When rest becomes a top priority for us, we're able to focus and think more clearly, casting off unnecessary burdens and stresses that make us weary. Our relationship with God grows stronger, and our load becomes lighter.

12

I'm Not OK, You're Not OK, But That's OK With God

50.0 million people have social phobias
21.5 million have sexual addiction disorder
15.0 million are depressed/anxious
14.0 million are alcoholics
10.0 million have borderline personality disorder
10.0 million have seasonal affective disorder
8.0 million have an eating disorder
5.4 million have obsessive-compulsive behavior
2.0 million are bipolar
.5 million have chronic fatigue syndrome
55.6 million have assorted other mental disorders

193.0 million Americans are dysfunctional—80% of the population.

As heard on the "Dr. Laura Show," July 22, 1998

This is a crazy world we live in. Even our pets can be dysfunctional. No joke—I read about a dog that was put on an antidepressant so he would quit running around in circles trying to eat his tail. I also know a veterinarian who gave Prozac to a bird so it would stop mutilating itself— "Polly Want a Prozac?"

How God Will Bless the Thorns in Our Flesh

My friend Karen says that she believes God directs into our lives one or two or more themes that break us down, make us weak, and bring us to a place where we cry out for something. She adds that these themes are broken humanity revealing itself. I add that I think she's right.

In Chapter Six I mentioned my pastor friend who suffers from panic attacks, an intense anxiety state causing extreme fear and anguish, producing physical symptoms such as choking and shortness of breath. A) The pastor has gone to the emergency room on several occasions due to his symptoms resembling a heart attack. My friend believes his disorder is part of God's unfolding plan for his life; that his thorn has allowed him to comfort and help those with similar conditions. Thomas Jefferson said, "Who then can so softly bind up the wound of another as he who has felt the same wound himself?"

Don't Come One Step Closer

These mental wounds aren't an easy subject to discuss. Even though mental illness is prevalent in society, with as many as one in four or five families affected,[1] many mental health patients are reluctant to reveal their condition for fear of rejection and shame. B)

I know a woman in her forties who feared telling her preteen-age children about her hospitalization for depression. She thought the disclosure might scare them as much as it scared her. This was her first experience with mental illness and she had little understanding of her problem. Prior to her depression, she admitted that she would have kept her

---

A) One particularly frightening thing about panic attacks is that in most cases they're not triggered by anything. It is not uncommon for a person to have been under a great deal of stress, and then during a time when they are not stressed, they suddenly experience a massive outpouring of adrenaline. Their symptoms include a rapid heart beat, difficulty breathing, a sinking feeling in the pit of the stomach, sweaty palms, and trembling. The first time people have this experience they think they're going crazy, having a heart attack, or at least losing control.

B) People of faith who come for counseling or therapy often suffer doubly. First, there is the discomfort of their anxiety or depression. Second, there is the feeling of defeat that they should even need help. They may have been told that their faith should be strong enough to help them through difficult times; there should be no need for professional help or any special medications. "Explanations" may be given for the person's problems that suggest he or she simply has some unconfessed sin, lacks some spiritual experience, or must be an inadequate believer; otherwise he or she would not be experiencing such problems. Now such a person not only has the distress of the original problems, but also has the extra guilt and defeat of feeling terribly inferior.

---

distance from a mentally ill person: "Don't you dare come one step closer—you're depressed!"

We're All Gonna Be OK

To present a cross section of issues or thorns that show how different and complex our individual brains are, I asked relatives, business clients, and acquaintances to share their experiences. Note to you all: Thanks for sharing. You guys are OK.

Sleep-Deprived, Depressed, and All Stressed Up

I have admired my older brother Rex ever since I quit hating him when I was seventeen. I always thought he was smart, funny, and had a rock-solid brain. I still think that. But a few years ago he confided in me that he had suffered from mild depression for years. And it was due to a strange cause: sleep apnea. This condition can be serious because the person frequently snores and involuntarily holds his breath, thus depriving the brain of oxygen. The sleep apnea sufferer may wake up several hundred times a night, yet have no memory of doing so.[2] At a sleep disorders clinic, my brother was told that the lack of oxygen to his brain over twenty years was enough to cause mild depression. He now wears a device over his nose and sleeps better, except for the night his puppies ate his sleep apnea device. Rex was dog-tired the next morning.

This same brother once came home from the hospital after a panic attack in his body, rather than his brain. A severe rash covered him from head to toe, causing intolerable itching and pain. The cause of his problem was determined to be rooted in stress, which literally got "under his skin." The doctor told him that wherever our minds or bodies are the most vulnerable is where stress will attack.

Don't Panic—It's Just a Panic Attack!

"Julie" began having panic attacks in college after her brother died. Then she began having attacks in the car. She was too terrified to drive, so her husband chauffeured her to work for six months. He didn't understand her anguish and thought a happy thought would stop her attacks. She began throwing up every morning, lost thirty pounds, and quit going anywhere. Death was constantly on Julie's mind.

She underwent a complete physical, checked out fine, and then visited an anxiety disorder therapist. The therapist ascertained that Julie had experienced a meltdown due to an extreme number of major unresolved life stresses. The next visit was to a psychiatrist, who prescribed Xanax, a tranquilizer. Julie wanted to be as drug-free as possible however, so she never finished the bottle. She was determined to work through her panic attacks, took baby steps each day, and was eventually restored to full health. Julie also said she found a church home where she experienced a rebirth. "I believe my faith actually helps keep the [panic] attacks at bay," she said.

Aftershocks Treatment

Psychologists say earthquakes and other natural disasters, wars, and sexual abuse can bring on posttraumatic stress disorder in susceptible individuals.[3] I have a cousin who lives on the island of Guam, where she has survived almost-yearly typhoons, an epidemic of snakes, jungle fires, and the '94 earthquake; which severely damaged her home and forever changed her life. The earthquake and aftermath triggered my cousin's anxiety disorder. For a while she took Prozac and saw a therapist. At present, she is doing well, even after surviving another snake epidemic and severe hurricane damage to her business.

Fibro-Phobia and Fibromyalgia

Fibro-Phobia is not the fear of fibbing, or the fear of too much bulk in the diet. Fibro-Phobia is a fictional word I coined to describe my fear of contracting a painful, frequently debilitating disease called fibromyalgia, occurring mostly in women age thirty through sixty. I'm fibro-phobic because I semi-fit the profile of a woman at risk.

Fibromyalgia has a connection to abnormal brain chemistry—low serotonin levels—and is considered a form of arthritis, but with a more extensive list of symptoms: restless legs, sleep disturbances, depression, anxiety, various extremes of pain in as many as eighteen pressure points in the body, fatigue, and migraine headaches.[4] Fibromyalgia may coexist with chronic fatigue syndrome or mitral valve prolapse—a benign condition causing the heart to beat rapidly.[5]

I'm personally aware of eight women who have received the fibromyalgia diagnosis, each with varying levels of ability to function. Three things they have in common:

1. They were stressed out for a long period before being diagnosed.
2. They're all married, and six of the eight have communication problems with their spouses. However, this illness is not partial to married women—my psychiatric nurse friend Geni White treats several patients who are single women.
3. They were all given antidepressants, and their doctors and therapists told them to exercise regularly.

Hopelessly Addicted . . . To You

One prevalent addiction with the potential to consume a person's life as much as alcoholism and drugs, is codependency. If you mention the word in conversation, most people can't define it. So what is codependency? Can you say: *unhealthy relationship addiction?*[6] Almost everyone I know has been codependent at one time or another, including me.

I have a friend who's been a recovering codependent for several years. (Another friend was *hospitalized* for codependency.) My friend "Ethel" was insecure, had a fear of rejection, and needed to be needed: all the components necessary for a codependent relationship to materialize. So here comes "Lucy," Ethel's partner in codependent crime. As each year passed, Ethel felt like a python was squeezing her. Her mind was choking and her spirit was suffocating. She said it was so hard to break free from the relationship because she felt "in bondage" to Lucy. Ethel felt she needed to please Lucy at all cost—anything to keep her from becoming angry. Lucy, alternately, continued making excessive demands on Ethel's friendship. She wanted to "own" Ethel; have her all to herself. The turning point came after Ethel read the book *Please Don't Say You Need Me*, by Jan Silvius. Through extreme resolve, Ethel slowly but steadfastly detached from her friend. She confessed that the process was sometimes painful, but her freedom was well worth the effort.

I was sucked into a codependent marriage, seduced by thick, lush chest hair. But then I'd had codependent relationships my whole life, with both hairy and non-hairy chest-ers, so this was an understandable transition. Fred controlled me with regular outbursts of anger. His verbal nagging was chronic, and for years I wasn't able to respond in any way but fear. I blamed myself for his flare-ups.

Gary Smalley and John Trent, Ph.D., authors of *The Language of Love* (Pocket), explain it this way: "When you link a present message to a past experience or event, you take a direct path to a person's emotions, thereby multiplying the impact of that message." Each negative comment Fred made mushroomed in my brain. I couldn't see beyond my faults to recognize that Fred had issues. He dealt with frustration by trying to control his home environment. It wasn't until I dealt with my own issues through counseling that I learned to deal with his anger. And now I rarely buy a ticket to get on his emotional roller coaster. Instead, I use humor and my own "hot-ness" (*he* thinks I'm hot) to defuse his fuse, if you know what I mean.

In Their Write Minds

Various studies have found that writers suffer depression at rates ten-to-thirty times higher than the rest of the population. Psychiatrist Nancy Andreasen believes that creative artists are more susceptible to psychiatric disturbances due to being unnaturally sensitive to stimuli of all kinds, including pain, both from the outside and from within.[7]

I belong to a writers' online group and once took an informal poll about the writers' anxiety and depression experiences. I was especially interested in responses from a Christian perspective. Depressed writers beat out anxious writers by a slight margin, and women topped men two to one. Many of their stories exposed nerves still raw and wounded, and their pain ran deep.

One respondent with a heart condition was on medicine that caused mood swings. C) He experienced severe depression and started drinking, smoking, and forgetting his life-saving medicine. Through a worldwide prayer chain and counseling, he changed his behavior and was restored to mental health.

Another man preached to me: "Faith is the only medicine you need. Since you don't believe God will answer your prayers, I empathize with your need for medication."

I have great faith and God does answer my prayers. I thank God that He knows what I need.

God, Faith, and Biology in a Nutshell

These next few paragraphs explain everything you ever wanted to know about *Why We're Not OK*.

Biology trumps faith, more often than some of us would like to admit. For starters, we all die a physical death, no matter how much faith we have. Also, God *made* us the way we are, biology and all. He understands and knows every fiber and chemical of our beings. He knew we would have fragile little brains, tendencies towards nervous habits, ADD, alcoholism, depression, anxiety, weight gain, etc. He told Moses, who was anxious and whining about his inability as a public speaker: "Who gave man his mouth? Who makes him deaf or mute? Who gives him sight or makes him blind? Is it not I, the Lord? Now go, I will help you speak and will teach you what to say" (Exodus 4:11-12).

Another reason we may struggle with physical and emotional issues: God wants to use every bit of who we are, including our gifts, talents, and flaws, to showcase His purposes. Anita Renfroe, in her book *If It's Not One Thing, It's Your Mother* (NavPress Publishing Group), shares her view: "Everything is not going to get fixed and healed in this lifetime. That's what Heaven is for."

C) Certain types of medication used for reasons other than mental illness can cause mood swings in a person—for instance, some blood pressure medications. Also, if an individual has a bipolar illness (formerly called manic depression), and he is not treated with a mood stabilizer, but an antidepressant only, there is an increased risk he will have more mood swings. The antidepressant causes the cycle to spin even faster. All illegal mind-altering drugs, as well as the abuse of tranquilizers and alcohol, can cause mood instability.

The good news: Faith ultimately and completely wins over biology, but not until we are heaven bound, where we'll commune with Jay-sus, sporting our perfect bodies and brains. That's my sermon, and I'm stickin' to it. Amen.

Healing Words

Even the saints had their "thorns in the flesh." The Apostle Paul asked God to heal him of his thorn, but God said: "'My grace is sufficient for you, for my power is made perfect in weakness. Therefore I will boast all the more gladly about my weaknesses, so that Christ's power may rest on me. That is why, for Christ's sake, I delight in weaknesses, in insults, in hardships, in persecutions, in difficulties. For when I am weak, then I am strong.'"

2 Corinthians 12:9-10

Paul's thorn kept him from becoming conceited about his gifts and talents and showed God's strength perfected in his weakness. Paul brought the Gospel to the masses and kept the faith while undergoing beatings, stonings, shipwrecks, imprisonment, hunger, and fatigue, because of God's indwelling strength. If a thorn in the flesh was God's plan for the Apostle Paul, it then follows that we'll be pricked with a thorn or two in this life.

Remember this: We all have flaws and weaknesses. God may allow them for our humbling, or to show forth His mighty power, so that we know it's Him working in, and in spite of, ourselves. Continue to have faith that God will do a mighty work in your mind, body, and spirit.

13

From Worrywart to St. John's Wort

Fred and I are desperately trying to escape somebody or something. I am ahead of him, climbing an extremely tall, rickety ladder made of wood, plastic, and fabric. The ladder leans against a three-story house. As I step gingerly from one rung to the next, every other rung breaks off and falls to the ground. Fred tries to steady me. I finally make it to the third-story window, and remove the screen. I see a young woman inside. She notices my plight and comes to help. She removes the dresser that is against the window and pulls me in. The ladder begins to crumble, and Fred begins to stumble. In horror I see the ladder start to fall away from the house. With adrenaline pumping, I reach out, grab Fred's shoulder, and pull him and the ladder towards me, with the woman holding on to me. Fred grabs the window ledge, and the young woman and I pull him inside. We are safe.

Dream, May 10, 1997

In my dreams I believe I can interpret dreams. Gustavus Hindman Miller thinks he can too. In his book *10,000 Dreams Interpreted*, he says this about "ladder" dreams: "To escape from captivity or confinement by means of a ladder you will be successful, though many perilous paths may intervene." Let me intervene here with: Hey! That is almost precisely the conclusion I came to about my ladder dream, with one difference. In my dream Fred and I did not escape until we were dead. We achieved complete success *posthumourously* as it were—laughing our heavenly heads off that we got away.

Dreams can be confusing, and so can their interpretations. Perhaps this explanation will help clarify. Fred and I are escaping from the anxiety and pain of life. The wobbly ladder symbolizes our perilous path to peace of mind. The fabric, plastic, and wood are temporary, fleeting answers to our lack of peace. They represent unhealthy or healthy fixes to whatever ails our psyche: fixes like cigarettes, alcohol, caffeine, vitamins, minerals, herbs, exercise, friends, etc.

Each rickety step on the ladder reminds me of the many twists, turns, and setbacks on the path to peace of mind. As I reach the top of the ladder, I see more obstacles: the window screen and the dresser on the inside of the window. Fred and I work as a team, helping each other up the ladder. He supports me as I climb gingerly ahead of him. The young woman (angel?) and I then help save his life as he stumbles and swings backwards. Once we enter through the window and are in the safe place, which I believe is heaven, the temporary solutions and obstacles fall away.

The Mental Obstacle Course We Call the Brain

For the last several years, Fred's hobby has been the brain. Nothing fires up his neurons more than attending brain conferences. When Emory University in Atlanta hosted *"Brain Awareness Week,"* Fred and I—always looking for a good time—went to a seminar on ADD.

While at the seminar, a woman and I discussed her ADD and my anxiety. She wondered if ADD, rather than anxiety, could be my problem. She said, "You should try Ritalin." Ritalin worked for her, so I should take it. She wasn't focusing on the fact that she and I might be just a wee bit different inside our heads.

For every person who's told me, "you should take this," there's another who says: "you shouldn't take this—it made my brother start clucking like a chicken and grow feathers." One person's negative or positive experience is not necessarily another's. A)

Through a contact at the seminar, Fred took part in a study that would determine conclusively if he indeed had ADD. Indeed, he did. Fred scored

---

A) A medication may work for one person but may have undesirable effects for another. The narcissistic myth goes: "if it's good for me, it's good for anyone else." This is a commonly held–and hazardous–belief.

a high IQ on the verbal parts of the test, but he scored low in the sections on processing information and working memory. This is a typical profile for a person with ADD, the study coordinator told him.

Fred continues to read about the brain. His favorite brain book is *The Emotional Brain* by Joseph LeDoux. Studying brain biochemistry is great therapy for Fred. He became so cerebral that when we'd visit the psychiatrist, Fred would tell Dr. C. about the material he read, what drug he thought he should take, and why:

"Dr. C., I don't believe my problem is as much a shortage of serotonin as it is a need for a boost of norepinephrine and/or possibly dopamine. I've also been studying ADD and feel that Wellbutrin might help my focus better than Serzone." Then they would both go off into brain-land, discussing PET (positive emission topography) scans and dopamine receptor sites. Meanwhile I sat there feeling dopey because I wasn't as cerebrally conversant as they were. I patiently waited for the symposium to end, bemused by Dr. Sigmund Fred.

Fred always tried to improve his focus, believing that his lack of clarity was the root of his depression and anxiety. As mentioned in an earlier chapter, at one time he experimented with caffeine pills and a few cigarettes a day. However, he lost his desire for the two daily cigarettes when he started taking the antidepressant Wellbutrin (Zyban). Wellbutrin is promoted as an anti-smoking drug, so for a depressed smoker Zyban might be doubly effective. Another plus for Wellbutrin: it doesn't depress the libido. B)

Don't Worry—Take Wort!

In June of '97, Fred watched the TV show *20/20*, which included a segment on St. John's Wort, an herb with the botanical name *hypericum*. Barbara Walters spoke of St. John's Wort as a natural remedy for anxiety and depression. Used in Germany for centuries, this herb was now

B) Depression very often results in sexual malfunction. As antidepressants clear depression, sexual function may improve. However, all antidepressants can cause sexual problems as a side effect. The two antidepressants least likely to cause sexual side effects are Wellbutrin and Remeron. 50-100 mg. of Viagra taken one hour before sexual activity has the highest success rate of correcting the sexual side effects of antidepressants, more so than any other intervention. Viagra can help women, as well as men.

available in the U.S. St. John's Wort, also known as SJW, or the "Wort," as I call it, had few side effects, was natural, and didn't require a doctor's prescription. The latest literature reports that St. John's Wort works best for mild depression or anxiety.

Of note: Dr. James Mallory, psychiatrist, prefers SAM-e, another over the counter alternative medicine, to SJW. He also recommends that patients check with their doctors if they're currently being treated for anxiety or depression, before starting SAM-e or SJW. Mixing certain drugs with St. John's Wort and quitting antidepressants or tranquilizers cold turkey is dangerous. C)

Fred, convinced that the Wort was for real, purchased a bottle at the health food store. He made sure the label said *"certified potency."* We gradually quit taking our prescribed antidepressants and started on the Wort. After nine days, I felt wonderful and so did Fred. We made our annual trek up north, and for the first time in years I didn't take a prescription tranquilizer for sleep. The SJW was working better than expected. I went to a reunion of a few high school friends and told them about the Wort. They were quite interested. Turns out that five of the six women were taking antidepressants or tranquilizers for either a mood disorder or hormone imbalance.

I considered my trip the acid test for SJW, and decided to write a post on one of the Internet anxiety sites about my experiences. One woman said she took St. John's Wort on my recommendation, and for the first time in a long time she spoke in public without having a panic attack. She felt an overall calmness that she hadn't experienced in years.

The only side effects I noticed from the Wort: a mild rise in my normally low blood pressure, and I grew a couple of warts from the Wort. I am not making this up. I was initially worried about my warts, but they have since disappeared.

C) There are many unproven and downright fraudulent claims made by various manufacturers and health food stores regarding the benefits of alternative medications for mental illness. Approximately 30 percent of all people will have some positive response to anything they are given (the placebo effect). There are some alternative medicines that have good research behind them that can help some diseases. EPA (Omega-3 Fatty Acid), at the dose of 1000 mg. a day, has shown value in stabilizing depression; SAM-E, supplemented by B12 and folic acid, has also helped some types of depression. Valerian and melatonin have been of value in helping people sleep. Kava Kava and St. John's Wort have been helpful to some, but they can be dangerous if combined with certain other medications. Meditation, replacing negative thinking with positive thoughts, and exercise have also shown to be helpful.

I spoke with Dr. Bigelow at the National Institutes of Mental Health about SJW. He told me that cows broke out with skin rashes after grazing a few too many weeks on St. John's Wort plants. But the cows probably weren't worried about their skin after digesting all that Wort. Mellow Cow Disease as opposed to Mad Cow Disease?

If Barbie Is So Popular, Why Do We Have to Buy Her Friends?

The healthiest among us find solace in companionships.[1] Fred didn't pursue solid friendships until he went through his severe depression. During his recovery, he expressed his feelings more openly. His buddies listened patiently to his chronic, negative self-talk.

Within a few months, Fred dropped the negative self-talk and became himself. Fred's self is melancholy, satirical, and full of dry wit. His unique sense of humor is one of his charms. And now he's gained cyber friends through a few online forums and support groups.

To keep up my relationship quota, I walk with a friend, play tennis, call or email friends, or eat lunch with favorite business clients. People energize me, but they also drain me, so I strike a balance between my alone time and people time.

One friend and I agreed that whenever one of us was going through a tough spot and life got messy, we'd leave a roll of toilet paper on the other person's doorstep, a more mature and less annoying gesture than rolling the other person's house. The toilet roll symbolized our willingness to support each other while we cleaned up the mess in our lives.

Author Ann Lamott sums up friends this way: "Of immeasurable value: People who see the dark, tricky broken parts of you, but love you anyway."

William Arthur Ward said: "A true friend knows your weaknesses but shows you your strengths; feels your fears but fortifies your faith; sees your anxieties but frees your spirit; recognizes your disabilities but emphasizes your possibilities."

Frederico's Oil

The movie *Lorenzo's Oil* ('92) is the true story of a little boy who was dying of leukoadrenodystrophy. This devastating, somewhat rare disease eats away at the body's myelin sheath, causing paralysis, blindness, and death to young males. The parents refused to accept the doctors' diagnosis of eventual death for their child. Instead, they took turns caring for him and researched at various libraries and chemical companies until they found a possible cure—a type of fatty acid or oil. They presented their research to a company in Great Britain, which processed the oil for human consumption. The oil halted the disease in their son and caused a substantial improvement in his condition.

My "Frederico's Oil" story is not in the same league with *Lorenzo's Oil*, but it is still significant. Olive oil and fish oil made such a difference in Fred's life that I'm sharing what he found.

One of the books Fred read in his quest for understanding and healing his brain was *The Zone*, by Dr. Barry Sears (HarperCollins). He wanted to see if being in the zone would lower his still-high liver enzymes, and if the food combinations would improve his mental clarity. The diet lowered his enzymes, but he also lost weight. Fred didn't need to be any leaner and meaner. Also, Fred was disappointed that *The Zone* kept him in the twilight zone mentally. His ability to focus did not change. He reread the book in '98 and decided he might need more fat in his diet. That bit of information led him to *The Omega Plan*, by Artemis P. Simopoulos and Jo Robinson (HarperCollins).

The Omega Plan convinced him that good fat was the solution to many of his ADD problems. He was so excited he wrote author Jo Robinson. She responded with her view that "if people would just start adding the right fats to their diet, we might eliminate most mental disorders in the country." She added that right fats include fish oil, flaxseed oil, olive oil, canola oil, Brazil nuts, and the fat found in salmon, tuna, cod, and mackerel. Ms. Robinson also wrote: ". . . fish oil may increase serotonin, the 'feel-good' hormone. One study used Omega-3 fatty acids as a treatment for bipolar disorder. The good fat caused remission in 60% of bipolar patients. The results were so promising the study was halted so the control group could benefit." D)

D) Regarding the above-mentioned study: The specific Omega-3 fatty acid that had this therapeutic effect is known as EPA. For EPA to have a therapeutic effect, people need 1000 mg. a day. I have added this regimen to some of my bipolar patients who have been poorly controlled; they are now doing much better. Further research has substantiated the initial study on the value of Omega-3 fatty acid. However, there is a pristine therapeutic window; less than 1000 mg. or significantly more fails to give the same effect.

A large portion of Fred's good fat comes from olive oil—virgin pressed. For years he drank a daily tablespoonful of olive oil, and he continues to take fish oil by the capsule. Since he does much of the cooking, we're on a Mediterranean, or Big Fat Greek diet. His ADD hasn't disappeared, but his good cholesterol is *very* good.

When guests come for dinner, Fred makes his special rigatoni and vegetable sauce cooked with olive oil. He serves a salad with olive oil, wine vinegar, garlic, and lemon dressing, five-plus seed bread with olive oil and garlic seasoning (broiled in the oven), and fresh fruit for dessert. Fred seems over-zealous about his olive oil, but then Popeye was overzealous about his Olive Oyl too.

Soothing Sensations

Since I love to eat, exercise is not an option; plus exercise offers great mental health benefits. Every day I sweat out those stress hormones through walking, tennis, or climbing steps. Years ago Dr. C. told me I needed to jog three miles, but I'm not crazy about running up and down the steep hills of my neighborhood. I *am* crazy about climbing up and down 200 steps of a wooded path I dug in my back yard though, sweating and smelling in total privacy. The reason I know I'm crazy is because I've seen snakes slithering along that path and I still climb it. When I don't feel like walking in the neighborhood or doing aerobics, I walk up and down my path with the snakes, twelve times, in forty minutes. (Actually, I don't know *how* fast the snakes go; I just know I go faster.) When I'm through, my legs feel like jello, but I *am* mellow.

There are many paths to mellow-ness. Supposedly, chewing gum or doing repetitive motions with your legs or body has a calming effect.[2] And if you can do both at the same time; well, you're a tranquil show off.

These next few paragraphs are going to sound weird.

I like to relax by turning on the TV and finding Jan Crouch, the platinum blonde lady on TBN. She soothes me as much as Mr. Rogers reruns soothe kids. If Fred switches channels and catches her, he'll call me. "Hey Shel, Jan is on!" I'll drop what I'm doing, run into the den and stare at her, hypnotized. Something about her voice calms me.

When I'm at the mall, I like to sit in a beauty salon and watch stylists cut customers' hair. Blow-drying especially lowers my heart rate. In department stores, I roam around looking for employees folding shirts or towels. Watching the repetitive motion is so relaxing. Interestingly, when *I* fold shirts or towels, the soothing sensation is lacking.

Other miscellaneous and more normal things I do for my brain: take high-potency vitamins, sleep eight or nine hours at night, pace myself, keep up with the latest research on the brain—via Fred, and laugh a lot.

Yeah I'm weird, and that's OK.

Healing Words

"But our citizenship is in heaven. And we eagerly await a Savior from there, the Lord Jesus Christ, who by the power that enables him to bring everything under his control, will transform our lowly bodies so that they will be like his glorious body."

Philippians 3: 20-21

Something to look forward to: our lowly bodies and brains being transformed into perfect and glorious bodies, by the power of Jay-sus!

"Carry each other's burdens, and in this way you will fulfill the law of Christ." Galatians 6:2

God created us not only for Himself, but also for each other. When we're at a low point in our lives, it's good to have emotionally and spiritually supportive people around to lift us up. Their healing words and deeds will be a tremendous blessing to us. And may we pass it on.

14

Idiot's Guide to the Brain

Human progress has never been achieved with unanimous consent. Those who are enlightened first are compelled to pursue the light in spite of others.

Christopher Columbus, 1492

The '90s, called the Decade of the Brain, brought forth enormous progress in understanding brain function. Researchers move closer each day to unlocking the mysteries of the brain. Hope is on the horizon for those still lacking successful treatment.[1]

Those who say mentally ill people should *just deal with it*—something they'd *never* tell a cancer patient—will be able to see physical proof of clinical depression, anxiety, attention deficit disorder, obsessive-compulsiveness, schizophrenia, etc., through the use of sophisticated brain scans.[2] Brain scans may one day be as common as ultrasounds or MRIs, and will help greatly in choosing various treatment options.[3]

Another possibility: *"Blue genes"* (my term) may be discovered for depression. Recently, an anxiety gene—a variation of a normal gene—was found. Scientists are calling it a personality gene that may influence a person's anxiety levels.[4]

Mesocortical *What?*

Since this chapter is "Idiot's Guide to the Brain," with me as the idiot, I won't fill it with charts and terms like "mesocortical dopaminergic system." I'll try to keep the brain-related words to a maximum of four syllables. I'm including my all-time favorite brain questions and will zero in on how certain questions apply to my and others' experiences. I'll include a little about the workings of the chemical brain, which may help explain why twenty-five percent of the population will encounter mental illness at some point during their lives.[5] If you want a deeper understanding of brain chemistry than what I've presented, see the notes and list of resources in the back of the book.

BRAIN QUESTION NUMBER 1: IS ALL MENTAL ILLNESS IN OUR GENES?

Beats me, but Carol Hart might have a clue.

Ms. Hart, author of *Secrets of Serotonin,* explains: "Chemistry + Events = Mood + Behavior." She writes that our genes and hormones program our tendencies. A) Our daily experiences and environment *influence* those tendencies. In her book, Ms. Hart explains the functions of serotonin, my favorite brain chemical, and one of the key chemicals responsible for mental wellbeing.

Ms. Hart says we can choose a lifestyle that increases our serotonin level. *What—like entering a monastery?* The calm, tranquil environment of monk-hood would certainly be conducive to a lifestyle of less stress and more serotonin. That might have been a good idea for much of my life, but I've never looked that great in brown. Plus, I burned out from bread baking years ago, and the wine cellars would have been too tempting. And let's not even talk about the vow of silence.

My second option after eliminating a cloistered lifestyle was to alter my non-cloistered lifestyle. I have learned to say no to certain invitations or requests, and try to choose my friends and clients wisely. Additionally, when I feel anxious, I chill. I don't rev up the anxiety engines and plan a big party or a huge convention, for instance. I'm not a workaholic, although I easily could be.

A) In terms of genetics and mental illness, the prevailing view is that there is an interaction between the two. If a person's genetic vulnerability to a particular mental illness is strong enough, no external stress whatsoever is required to produce symptoms. Vulnerable people will, unless treated, continue to have symptoms all their lives. If the genetic vulnerability is minimal, it may take a catastrophe to trigger symptoms. But once triggered, less and less outside stress is required to cause the next depressive or anxious episode. Attacks tend to beget more attacks.

If I didn't have tendencies towards anxiety, I wouldn't need to work so hard at managing my brain. I know that by making wise decisions I can help maintain my mental health. My brain is either my friend or my enemy. My *mind* would like my *brain* to cooperate so I could be fun-loving, extroverted, and spontaneous every waking moment. But it seems my brain's amygdala, the probable fear center, kicks in with, "Fear, fear, alarm, alarm! Danger, danger, Will Robinson!"

My friend "Sophie" was a physical and mental wreck due to the conflict between her mind and her brain. She became a registered nurse at age forty-five. A full-time nursing career can be full-time stress for any age nurse, but especially for someone entering the field in her forties. Sophie's personality, desire, and mind blended well with nursing, but her sensitive brain and body said, "I don't think so!" She worked double shifts, nights, and weird hours, upsetting her fragile body rhythm.

After a few years on the job, she injured her back from helping lift a 600-pound man. She took one year's disability. During this off time, her monthly migraines worsened and no longer responded to self-injected shots of a strong pain reliever. She was on two medications for sleep, and took two more for digestive problems.

Sophie visited me in the midst of her nursing career crisis. When I picked her up at the airport, her first words were, "I'm fried bacon!" My unsolicited advice was that she leave the hospital environment altogether. She did, and is much improved.

BRAIN QUESTION NUMBER 2: HOW IS FEAR GENERATED?

I'm afraid I don't know.

But Fred has a theory, which you may or may not agree with, based upon his reading of *The Emotional Brain* by Joseph LeDoux. His review of LeDoux's book on www.amazon.com:

The implications of LeDoux's book are enormous. LeDoux, a neuroscience researcher, shows that our emotions are generated by separate independent neuro systems which work unconsciously. Believe it or not, we do NOT run because we are afraid, but rather we are afraid because we run. He also shows that the emotional systems have a much greater impact on our rational conscious than the rational conscious has on the emotional systems. Passion rules reason. This has tremendous implications for the current thinking in psychology/psychiatry (although they [mental health professionals] will be slow to pick up on it). And it explains why man has so much angst, why we don't learn from history, why man is so brutal. The importance of this book cannot be overstated.

Dr. Joseph LeDoux gave the example of "freezing" as the first reaction people have when afraid or in sudden danger. They freeze without thinking. He said the Atlanta Olympic Park bombing was a good illustration of this: "The bomb goes off and everyone hunches over in the freezing posture for a couple of seconds, and then they take off running. You can almost see the cognitive gears turning while they're freezing . . . we're not in direct control of these rapid fire, unconscious, emotional responses . . ."

Dr. Michael Davis, Ph.D., a professor of psychiatry at Emory University involved in anxiety research, said it's quite difficult to suppress unwanted fear memories. He said, "We probably never forget our fear, as the incidents powerfully imbed themselves into the brain by the stress chemicals that are released. The extinction process for fear memories is quite fragile. We can learn to cope with those memories, however."[6]

BRAIN QUESTION NUMBER 3: WHY DOES THERAPY TAKE SO LONG TO WORK?

I'd ask my therapist, but I'm no longer seeing him. However, my favorite psychologist, Dr. Melanie Wilson, states:

Learning new habits requires new connections in the brain. Sometimes those new connections can be forged quickly. For example, only one time of petting the neighbor's dog will be required for you to learn not to pet him if he bites you. The negative consequences of your action are experienced swiftly and painfully. But learning not to overeat will likely take longer. The consequences are not immediate and not nearly as painful in the moment. Psychotherapy is more like learning not to overeat than it is not to pet the vicious dog. Like drug therapy, therapy requires time to correct brain chemistry and change the way our brains function. However, the most effective treatments for mental illness usually incorporate both medication and therapy. So be a patient patient!

Of course, the less severe the psychological problem, the greater the probability for an easier cure. Case in point: About ten years ago ago I suffered mild postpartum depression—over my neighbor bringing twin babies home from the hospital. That sounds far-fetched even to me, so let's refine that diagnosis and label it mild posttraumatic stress disorder, most likely catalyzed from my angst-filled memories of sleepless nights with a newborn. I began worrying about my neighbor. *How will Carrie get any sleep caring for those babies? If she doesn't sleep, she'll freak and throw both babies and herself out the window! They're all going to die! ACCCHHHHH!*

Obsessing about poor Carrie and her babies, I superimposed my anguished thoughts onto her. (By the way, my neighbor is totally OK in every way, and she handled the twins with no problem, never once losing her mind. I was more stressed than she was.)

I felt worthless and useless for a few days due to my excessive emotional expenditure on Carrie and her twins, but I masked my symptoms quite well. I finally told Fred I was feeling crummy. Fred transformed into his alter ego, "Dr. Sigmund Fred," and we had a cognitive therapy/psychoanalysis session. Dr. Fred told me to write down my feelings, and then asked me to respond logically to each piece of emotional distress I listed. Talking about and writing out my thoughts and fears helped me get my brain back so my mind could think rationally.

BRAIN QUESTION NUMBER 4: WHY DOES IT TAKE SO LONG FOR ANTIDEPRESSANTS TO WORK?

Theories abound. Perhaps in this millennium scientists will figure out the answer.

Dr. Clint Kilts, Associate Professor of Behavioral Science at Emory University, met with me and shared: "The brain's slow response time to the effect of antidepressants relates to the 'cumulative neural adaptive response.' The brain doesn't automatically get healthy just because it's had a dose or two of an antidepressant. It usually must accumulate several hits before the antidepressant kicks in. If the correct antidepressant has been taken, the brain eventually (in two to six weeks' time) adjusts from a state of depression or anxiety to emotional stability."

Even though our brains are slow to absorb antidepressants, Dr. Kilts added that the brain is still the most malleable and plastic organ we own, as indicated by the amazing strides made by some patients whose brains are damaged by strokes.

BRAIN QUESTION NUMBER 5: WHY DO WOMEN SUFFER FROM DEPRESSION MORE THAN MEN DO?

Maybe women get depressed more because their depressed husbands won't seek help, and that depresses them.

Some researchers say that women utilize serotonin (helps regulate mood) differently than men do.[7] Women also pursue treatment for their depression more readily than men do, which could skew the statistics for male and female depression. B) As the stigma declines and information grows, mental health professionals think that we'll continue to see a narrowing of the gap between rates for male and female depression.[8]

BRAIN QUESTION NUMBER 6: WHAT HAPPENS TO A YOUNG CHILD'S BRAIN WHEN EXPERIENCING INTENSE PAIN AND FEAR?

I have no idea, but it can't be good.

According to Dr. James Dobson, founder of *Focus on the Family,* those unfortunate children produce high levels of stress hormones that put the body into a perpetual alarm reaction state. The child's brain is bombarded with stress chemicals, causing the thinking mechanisms and emotional development to become impaired.

"Many of today's abused kids are literally brain-damaged," adds Dr. Dobson. "They can't empathize with helpless victims the way they should, because the emotion of compassion flows from cognitive functions that no longer operate."[9]

B) Current research shows that women are prone to depression 1.5 times more often than men. There are many unproven theories as to why women are more prone to depression. Some theories include hormone imbalance, culture, and abuse. However, men are four times as likely to commit suicide as women. Apparently, women are better able to endure the psychic pain of depression. Men will often not hang in long enough with a doctor to get on the right treatment at the right dose, because of the old masculine ego. Some won't want to admit defeat; they want to overcome the problems on their own.

I've read that a majority of prisoners were raised fatherless and suffered neglect and abuse as children. Countless thousands of those inmates have suffered from a mental illness since childhood, and many entered prison during their teen years, or even younger.[10] Yet prison is "a perilous prescription" for their treatment. Due to lack of good mental health programs and funding in many states, there is often nowhere else for the wayward mentally ill child to go but behind bars.[11]

Zero Tolerance

Even if we never get to the bottom of our brains, at the very least may we be aware that mental illness is as real and as formidable a foe as cancer or diabetes, only with a stigma attached.

David Satcher, former U.S. Surgeon General and a strong proponent for mental health parity, believes that stigma is a barrier that discourages individuals from getting treatment: "There's no longer justification for distinguishing between mental and physical illnesses—because there are physical, chemical bases for mental illnesses. We hope that will help to change the stigma that so often surrounds mental illness and therefore make it easier for people to seek treatment."[12]

What we should *not* tolerate is the stigma. Stigma is *Not OK*.

Healing Words

"Trust in the Lord with all of your heart, and lean not on your own understanding; in all your ways acknowledge him, and he will make your paths straight." Proverbs 3:5-6

When we've made up our minds without consulting the One who made our minds, we risk going against the grain of God's will for us. Our stubbornness to see things our way only can lead to serious emotional setbacks. God will show us the way if we let Him—and all His ways lead towards inner peace.

"For he has rescued us from the dominion of darkness and brought us into the kingdom of the Son He loves, in whom we have redemption, the forgiveness of sin." Colossians 1:13-14

It's never too late to be rescued, to have our minds and spirits restored. Even though we may feel that we've wasted months or years in a state of emotional and spiritual upheaval, God can still meet us where we are today, right now. God is greater than our past and our present, and He desires to redeem our future.

15

We're OK With God

Every day brings a chance to live free of regret and with as much joy, fun, and laughter as you can stand.

Oprah Winfrey

Gone With the Wind

In January 2000, I was at the Super Bowl in Atlanta as a volunteer. The Super Bowl should have been a proud moment for me, as my daughter was a musician performing in the Disney halftime show. However, it was a stupid, humiliating, shameful moment for me. More like the Stupid Bowl.

During halftime, we volunteers were allowed to sit on the Tennessee Titans bench to watch the show, and several from our group—which included college students, a few adults, and me, whatever *I* am—thought it might be fun to lift a Gatorade towel as a souvenir. The Gatorade halftime heist may have been a typical college prank, but it was not a typical, middle-aged woman prank. I do not know what caused my temporary lapse of sanity. For some reason, that overly used excuse—"But Mom, the other kids were doing it!"—just didn't seem to work.

My timing didn't work either. The security people were decidedly fed up with fans helping themselves to souvenirs. As I was walking off the field, they caught me orange-handed, clutching my Gatorade towel. So I had to throw in the towel. I handed it to a big, burly security guy, who asked me sarcastically, "How OLD are you?" And I responded meekly, "Too old." Big Burly Guy, disgusted, told one of the guards to arrest me. I was going to be the scapegoat. Even though I was unbelievably remorseful and started crying, they persisted.

As they were taking me away to the Georgia Dome Dungeon to charge me with theft, I lost all control of bodily functions. I was so upset. And very wet and very cold.

But this is when God appeared, in a gust of wind. At that moment, an enormous rush of cold air blasted into the Georgia Dome wind tunnel, threatening to blow apart some very expensive twenty-foot-tall Disney puppets. The security guard left me to chase down the puppets, and he never came back. I didn't go looking for him either, although I was paranoid "they" were still after me for days.

When out driving I wore oversized sunglasses—in February—and with darting eyes checked my rearview mirror repeatedly for suspicious-looking unmarked cars driven by big, burly guys. I'm convinced I overreacted to this whole episode due to some severe, unrelated stress I was suffering from at the time: My mother was dying and had just a few weeks to live. I'm not blaming my stress for the theft—I do know it was wrong to lift the towel. But it was just as "wrong" for my brain to go haywire. Repentance and remorse would have sufficed. But that's OK, eight years later I can find the humor in the Gatorade Towel Heist.

Top Ten List

As I get older, I'm learning to steal less and laugh more. In fact, just about everything I've needed to know about mental health I've learned in menopause. Here's a Top Ten List of Midlife Mental Lessons Learned:

1. It's OK to admit when you're depressed, anxious, and/or stressed.
2. It's OK to become educated and change lifelong views held about mental illness.
3. It's OK to get help for emotional problems from a pastor, counselor, or doctor.
4. It's OK to realize we're all flawed and weak at various times.
5. It's OK to believe that there's healing to be found through faith, medicine, friends, laughter, and other avenues too numerous to mention.
6. It's OK to get rid of the shame and blame.
7. It's OK to be real and honest with yourself and others; just choose your "others" wisely.

8. It's OK to shed the commonly held belief that if all people just "pulled themselves up by their bootstraps" they'd overcome their mental problems.
9. It's OK to cling to God in desperation when the darkness won't disappear.
10. It's OK to laugh at ourselves and at life.

Good Grief/Bad Grief

When my mom passed away after a long bout with cancer, I leaned on family, friends, and faith to cope with the intense, powerful emotions. For eleven days after my mom's death I remained in an anxious, grief-stricken state. On the twelfth day the anxiety left abruptly, as did the grief. My fast track to grief healing sure wasn't anything I was controlling. Even though I was quickly recovering, I was curious about a series of grief support meetings being held in the area.

I went to one meeting, and one meeting only. Of all the group members, I had experienced the most recent death of a loved one, but I was also the most recovered. From listening to others' stories and comments, I gathered my rapid return to near-normalcy was due to my months of pre-grieving; plus, my grief was not complicated by guilt. The guilt burden weighed as heavy as the grief on some of the attendees.

One woman confessed that she had become severely depressed after her young son died. She said she knew suicide wasn't an option, because she'd lose her ticket to heaven. Upon hearing that comment, a father and his young adult daughter—who had recently suffered the loss of their daughter/sister—abruptly left the room, with the father appearing crushed and the daughter in tears. A) Grief—it can cause such . . . grief.

A) Many people who are severely depressed say the only reason they do NOT commit suicide is due to their belief in God. Most people (including Christians) who do commit suicide have the fixed, if not delusional belief, that they will never be well. They believe they are a burden to friends and family, and that everyone would be better off if they were dead. Sometimes depression is so severe that people develop false patterns of belief, such as: They have committed the unpardonable sin, or somehow are to blame for bad things happening in the world. Thus, the only solution is suicide. The person who is dominated by such a belief and commits suicide is not operating in a rational frame of mind or behavior. This desperate act may not reflect the individual's true spiritual status.

Update on Fred's Head (Or "SAM-e, How I Love Ya, How I Love Ya . . .")

My husband and his brain both retired from a thirty-year stint with the government a few years ago. Fred went off St. John's Wort and is currently on 1600 mgs. per day of SAM-e, another over-the-counter, all natural antidepressant. B) SAM-e is working well for Fred, even as he deals with some fairly serious physical problems. The best news is there are no known side effects, except for the fact that SAM-e can be somewhat expensive. (Fred's research found that NatureMade brand is the "gold standard" for SAM-e: the best quality at the best price. You can find it at www.drugstore.com.)

Fred also quit drinking, mainly as an experiment to see if his elevated liver enzymes would normalize. They didn't, but his depressed moods lifted. And Fred was not a heavy drinker—two glasses of wine per day was the norm. Fred highly recommends the "no alcohol" approach for everyone, especially those with a tendency towards depression.

On those occasions when he's visibly stressed, I continue to rub the middle of his forehead in a slow, circular motion. He said when I do that he usually experiences an almost instantaneous reversal of anxious and negative thoughts.

Fred still takes small doses of Adderal for his ADD, and he also ingests a plethora of drugs for his physical health. In 2004 he was diagnosed with primary sclerosing cholangitis—or PSC, a quite rare and serious autoimmune liver disease found to be the culprit behind his years of elevated liver enzymes. The disease progresses unpredictably, and the only cure is a liver transplant. We also speculate the liver disease may have contributed to his depression. Additionally, Fred developed UC—ulcerative colitis, in 2005. (A large majority of people with PSC also develop UC.) Despite the fatigue and other complications provoked by these diseases, Fred's life has been made more comfortable with no small thanks to the support of a fantastic online group consisting of PSC patients, caregivers, and medical experts.

B) Through documented research, SAM-e (acronym for S-Adenosyl-L-Methionine; a substance that occurs in the cells of plants, animals, and humans), has been shown to improve depression, especially when supplemented by vitamin B12 and folic acid.

Update on My Head

My daughter came home from college one day and told me that it was "National Anxiety Disorders Screening Day" on her campus. Her test results showed that she was "normal," with high self-esteem, a high confidence level, and had no major worries. She bragged to the screener, "Well, you ought to meet my mother."

So I went to her nearby campus and took the test. I was definitely feeling normal while answering the questions, especially since I was sitting next to a bipolar woman with anxiety and ADD. The woman was in her manic state and very vocal about her disorders.

After grading my test, the counselor/screener proceeded to tell me I had panic disorder. I was panic-struck. "I don't have panic disorder!" I argued with the counselor. Before she tacked on "oppositional defiance disorder," I walked out. Everyone has an opinion, and hers did not reflect my reality. My anxiety disorder had been under new and improved management for some time.

A couple of years ago, a pretty severe blip on the menopause radar surfaced, unfortunately coinciding with Fred's retirement. And let me just say that I strongly recommend *either* menopause *or* retirement for a couple considering their options, not both. I began jogging several times a week to counteract my emotional over-reactivity. The intense physical exercise helped to diffuse my anger and irritability at the government for allowing Fred to retire and intrude on my space.

However, my most amazing and recent treatment for emotional upheaval is calcium and magnesium. A few years ago I was diagnosed with osteopenia, and was put on a drug to increase bone density. I was also told quite forcefully that I HAD to increase my calcium intake if I didn't want to be a hunchback in about ten years. So I began taking 1200 mg. of calcium with vitamin D, and 500-600 mg. of magnesium per day. The calming effect of the calcium/magnesium helps me to sleep before, during, and after stress. I seriously wonder how different my life would have been if I'd taken the calcium/magnesium over the last twenty years. I can tell you this—the book title may have changed to "Take Calcium and Magnesium and You'll Be OK." In fact that's all there may have been—a book title.

Cracked Pots

"Cracked Pots" would have made another great book title, but Sunithi Gnanadoss already claimed a very similar title: "The Cracked Pot," for her charming Indian folk tale, which I've adapted here. I close with these words, which will compel you to hug yourself.

A water bearer in India had two large pots, each hung on an end of a pole that he carried across his neck. One of the pots had a crack in it, and while the other pot was perfect and always delivered a full portion of water to the master's house, the cracked pot arrived half full. For two years this went on daily, with the bearer delivering only one-and-a-half pots full of water to his master's house. Of course, the perfect pot was proud of its accomplishments. But the poor cracked pot was ashamed of its imperfection, and miserable that it was able to accomplish only half of what it had been made to do. After two years of what it perceived to be a bitter failure, it spoke to the water bearer one day by the stream.

"I am ashamed of myself, and I want to apologize to you."

"Why?" asked the bearer. "What are you ashamed of?"

"I have been able, for these past two years, to deliver only half my load because this crack in my side causes water to leak out all the way back to your master's house. Because of my flaws, you have to do all of this work, and you don't get full value from your efforts," the pot said.

The water bearer felt sorry for the old cracked pot, and in his compassion he said, "As we return to the master's house, I want you to notice the beautiful flowers along the path."

Indeed, as they went up the hill, the old cracked pot took notice of the sun warming the beautiful wild flowers on the side of the path, and this cheered it some. But at the end of the trail, it still felt bad because it had leaked out half its load, and so again the pot apologized to the bearer for its failure.

The bearer said to the pot, "Did you notice that there were flowers on your side of the path, but not on the other pot's side? That's because I have always known about your flaw, and I took advantage of it. I planted flower seeds on your side of the path, and every day while we walk back from the street, you've watered them. For two years I have been able to pick these beautiful flowers to decorate my master's table. Without you being just the way you are, he would not have this beauty to grace his house."

In other words, dear Cracked Pots and assorted lovable Crackpots: you've hit the jackpot. Your crooked cracks, crevices, and crannies have increased your worth, adding richness, mystery, and beauty to our world.

And that is *so* OK with God. He wouldn't have it any other way.

Now get crackin' and go water those flowers.

Healing Words ————————————————

"This is what the LORD Almighty says: 'Administer true justice; show mercy and compassion to one another . . . '"
Zechariah 7:9a

When we're hurting, we're sometimes insensitive to the hurts of others. It's "all about us." But it's really all about Him. And His desire is for us to develop a heart of mercy, as well as a discerning mind, especially while in the presence of other hurting people. Our words will not only contribute to their healing process, but to ours as well.

"Though he brings grief, he will show compassion, so great is his unfailing love." Lamentations 3:32

God loves us through our grief and heartache, understanding all of it. We sense His presence through the touch of a hand, the warmth of a smile, the words from a loved one, and the quietness of our own thoughts. In our fragility and weakness, we gain His strength and move on.

It's OK to Write Your Notes Here

Mental Notes

By Melanie Wilson, Ph.D.

The below notes reference topics discussed in *I'm Not OK, You're Not OK, But That's OK With God*. For further mental health information, see the list of recommended resources and notes at the back of the book.

ADD

When someone you know has ADD, love the person as he is, accepting that he may never change. Help your family member determine strategies for coping with organizational challenges. When positive changes are made, praise them.

Addictions

If you are battling an addiction, find a support group. There are likely Twelve Step programs in your area. If not, check out an online support group or contact one of the organizations listed on the Resources page at the back of the book.

Anxiety

- Take note of the situations that cause you the most anxiety. You will have a long-term goal of managing these situations with help.
- Develop anti-anxiety rituals. Try a number of different activities when anxiety is high and see what is most effective. We're all different, but walking, praying, talking it out, and deep breathing are popular remedies.
- Give your worries away. You can deposit your worries in an online worry bank, hire a professional worrier, or ask someone to pray for you. Present your prayer request at www.prayforyou.com and take comfort in knowing that someone is praying for you daily for a week.
- Take control of worries. Make a list of every worry on your mind. Across from each worry, list what action you will take. The action could be to put it on the calendar to deal with later, to ask for help, to pray, or to take a step toward solving a problem. Taking action will decrease your anxiety level.

Communication and Relationships

- Be honest about your mental illness. Almost everyone you know has faced emotional trauma. Talking openly is the best way to alleviate shame.

- Do you have family members who have a mental illness? Do a little research to find out more about your family's mental health history.

- Talk to your spouse so he can hear. How is your husband or wife most likely to understand what you're going through? Decide whether to talk about it, write about it, or have her read about it. Would reading and talking about this book together help? Some spouses may appreciate getting more information from a support group or mental health professional

- Do you have a need to hide the real you? Getting involved in a small group that encourages confidentiality may give you the security you need to tell the truth. Pour out your real feelings to God in prayer or in a journal. Ask Him to provide you with a trustworthy confidant.

- Develop and nurture friendships. A loving gesture toward someone who seems even more insecure than you may blossom into a wonderful relationship. Regularly call, visit, write to, and have fun with friends. If you are going through an especially difficult period emotionally, ask for prayer or assistance. Be willing to receive as well as give.

- Consider friendships carefully. Friendships that motivate you to be your best are healthy. Friendships that encourage dependence (in either direction) are not healthy. Do you feel better or worse about yourself in your friendship? If you feel better, chances are you have a healthy relationship. However, take the concerns of spouses and counselors regarding friendships very seriously.

Depression

- Screen yourself for depression. If you believe you are depressed or if you have at least five of the following symptoms each day for two weeks or longer, consult a mental health professional:

  - Feeling sad, down, or irritable for most of the day
  - Inability to enjoy activities that once brought pleasure
  - Significant changes in appetite and/or weight
  - Persistent feelings of guilt, hopelessness, or worthlessness

- Difficulty concentrating, remembering, or making decisions
- Fatigue
- Restlessness or slowed responses
- Feeling preoccupied with death or suicide

- Discuss postpartum depression with your physician. If you have a newborn, ask for help. Let someone else watch the baby while you rest, exercise, or get out of the house. Talk with other moms about what you're feeling.

Dreams

Explore your dreams. Dreams are not always prophetic and are not always indicative of secret desires. Dreaming that your child drowns does not mean it will happen. Dreaming of an affair does not mean you are longing for one. Sometimes dreams can be very informative, however. If you would like to make the most of your dreams, have a pen and paper next to your bed and record everything you can remember from your dreams immediately upon awakening. Remember that not recalling any dreams is also completely normal. Some symbols that appear in dreams may have specific meaning. If you dream you are in a tornado or hurricane, you are probably feeling stressed or overwhelmed, for example. Dream dictionaries can be helpful in searching for the meaning of such symbols. Other times dreams are simply a conglomeration of many things you have seen or heard or thought recently. Your brain is processing the information and the result can be a strange, but relatively meaningless dream.

Exercise

Begin a regular exercise program with your doctor's approval. Exercise is beneficial for many mental and physical afflictions. You could start with just ten minutes of walking, three days a week. Make your exercise time enjoyable by walking with someone or listening to music.

Laughter

- Make time for fun and laughter. Do something every day for a laugh: read the comics, watch a funny movie, play a practical joke, make funny faces with your kids. Set aside time in your weekly schedule for recreation.

- Cultivate your sense of humor. Humor that's relevant to what you're experiencing will be most likely to relieve stress. So reading this book is good for you!

Loss and Grief

Learn the difference between grief and depression. Grief is a normal response to a loss. The loss could be of a person, a pet, a home, a job, or anything that was of great value. Explore past losses through journaling, reading, support groups, and psychotherapy.

Our culture is very uncomfortable with grief. Because of this discomfort, medications are prescribed and mental illness labels are inappropriately given. Expressing grief is a normal and healthy reaction. An effort to stop tears or pretending as though no loss has occurred is likely to create mental illness. If you or someone you know is suicidal or completely unable to function for more than two weeks following a loss, treatment for depression (rather than simple grief) may be in order.

Medications, Herbs, and Supplements

- Consider whether herbal treatments for mental illness are right for you. Many people feel more comfortable taking natural supplements, and because they do, may experience relief from taking them. However, be advised that herbs are drugs too. You should tell your doctor and pharmacist that you are taking herbs and request that the doctor/pharmacist ascertain whether the herbs are safe for you. Educate yourself on the side effects and drug interactions of all the medications, herbs, and supplements you are taking.
- Consider whether or not to make medication part of your treatment plan. Psychotherapy alone can be just as effective as medication for some individuals. Taking medication without seeing a psychotherapist is effective for some. Still others experience the most benefit from the combination of psychotherapy and drug therapy. What is most important in determining your success is how you feel about treatment. For example, if you are frightened of medications or therapy, you are unlikely to benefit. You may wish to discuss treatment options with a psychotherapist and a psychiatrist. Understand that most psychiatrists prescribe medications and do not do psychotherapy, whereas

psychotherapists cannot prescribe medications. If you choose therapy and drug treatment, your two mental health providers will work together.

Mental Health Professionals

- Ask your doctor or therapist to tell you his/her perspective on mental illness and medication use. Consider seeing another professional if you do not feel supported in your approach to change.
- Schedule a thorough physical exam if you have not had one recently.
- Seek professional help if you have any questions or concerns. Even if you're feeling OK at the time of the appointment, you will probably feel the reassurance was worth the visit.
- Acknowledge that there is no one else like you. Your hurts are unique; your helps will be, too. Work with your doctor or counselor to find the treatment best suited to you physically, emotionally, and spiritually.
- Choose the right mental health professional. Seek a licensed provider who is covered by your insurance policy and who is supportive of your faith. The relationship is critical. If you aren't getting what you need, ask for a referral. A psychiatrist will prescribe medication, but is unlikely to do psychotherapy. A psychologist will do assessment and psychotherapy, but will not prescribe medication. Counselors and therapists will do talk therapy.
- Determine what, if any, form of psychotherapy is right for you. Some options to consider are:

  - Family or Couples Counseling: The philosophy is that change in any one individual can create change in a marriage or family. When counseling involves the whole family unit, resistance to change is less likely and rapid growth is often the result.
  - Behavioral Therapy: The philosophy is that changing thoughts changes emotions. Behavior change is believed to occur when the rewards for change outweigh its negative effects. Therapy is not talk-centered and is usually brief.
  - Psychoanalytic Therapy: Believes most mental illness has its roots in early experience. Analysis of subconscious material and the relationship between client and therapist is the focus of therapy. Usually treatment lasts several years.
  - Humanistic Therapy: Believes change is a result of listening to the

client and giving her unconditional positive regard. The therapist is much less directive than in other forms of therapy.

- Eclectic Psychotherapy: Most therapists consider themselves eclectic in approach, meaning they will draw from many different schools of thought and are willing to use a variety of techniques in assisting their clients. Spouses or family members may be brought in for some sessions, for example.

- In your first session with a psychotherapist, ask him or her to specify the approach to treatment being considered. Think about your reaction to the therapist. Sometimes negative reactions indicate that this particular therapist could help you work through unresolved issues. Other times, the reaction is so negative that it will hinder you from making progress. Find a therapist you can trust even if you have to meet with several.

Mental Illness in Children
Does your child's behavior give you cause for concern? If you observe ongoing disturbing or disruptive behavior, consult your pediatrician.

Music Therapy
Engage in music therapy. Musical notes have the power to relax us. Lyrics have the power to change our thoughts. Choose music that transports you to a higher place.

Nutrition
- Are there foods that trigger a feeling of being "out-of-control"? List them for now and later you can develop a plan for freedom in eating.
- Be serious about proper diet and exercise. Psychotherapy and psychoactive medications both change brain chemistry. But food and exercise do too and they're a lot less expensive. You'll be more likely to succeed in making positive fitness and nutrition changes if you make very small changes and if you make them with someone else.
- Instead of setting a goal to lose twenty pounds, make a plan to eat more fruit this week or ask a friend to take a ten-minute walk with you today. As you experience success, add another small and easily achievable goal.

Prayer and Spiritual Growth

- Ask others to pray that you will be protected from evil and then trust that God will answer that prayer. Some mental illnesses create confusion about spiritual issues. For example, people with schizophrenia sometimes believe they are God. If you are feeling confused, talk with a spiritual mentor or Christian psychotherapist about your experiences.

- Accept your trials as an opportunity for spiritual growth. People who have experienced mental illness in themselves or in someone they love grow in compassion and are unlikely to judge others. In your suffering, God will draw you nearer to Him and may use this time to teach others about loving through low times, too. Sometimes, the quicker we learn the lesson, the shorter the test.

- When someone you love has a mental illness, consider how God may be using this trial to change you. If you are willing, you can grow in patience and compassion. Be a source of encouragement to your loved one, and if you can't be, take time away to regroup.

- Give God control of your life and mental illness. Admitting you are powerless allows God to demonstrate His power through you. Praying, worshipping, and reading His word are the most effective ways of building trust so you can let go.

Sleep

Set a regular sleep and wake-up time to thwart insomnia. Consistency is as important as the amount of sleep you get. But make changes slowly by resetting your sleep clock ten minutes at a time. Engage in relaxing activities for the last hour before bedtime, and see a medical or mental health professional for assistance with persistent sleep difficulties.

Stress

- Conquer the control freak in you. Ask God to help you see your current difficulties as a reminder that you're not in charge. Thank Him for being in control and ask Him for help in trusting Him.

- If you are a stay-at-home mom with young children, for example, you experience more mental health challenges than many single working women. Determine whether your standards are higher than God's standards for you.

- Recognize when your expectations are unrealistic. Say, "I can't" when you're overwhelmed. Saying "no" can create more stress, so say, "I'd love to, but I can't." Don't spend a lot of time justifying yourself. You are important! Saying "I can't" may mean the difference between coping and crashing.

Suicide
- Know the suicide warning signs:

  - Talking about suicide
  - Saying things will never get better or people would be better off without him
  - Talking about death a lot
  - An abrupt change to being happier and at peace after a period of depression
  - Apathy about things that used to be important
  - Contacting friends and loved ones
  - Putting financial, funeral, and other affairs in order
  - Giving possessions to others

- If you are concerned, ask the person at risk if they have thought about suicide. If she has, ask her if she has a plan. If she is ready to take her own life and nothing will stop her, take her to an emergency room or call 911 for assistance. If she is not an immediate risk, warn friends and family members and remove items such as razor blades, medications, and guns from the home. Ask someone to stay with her, and if she is seeing a mental health professional, inform him as soon as possible. If you are the person considering suicide, tell someone now. A twenty-four-hour hotline is available at 1-800-SUICIDE.

Thoughts and Feelings
- Make a list of thoughts and behaviors you find difficult to control. This list will be valuable in setting up a behavioral treatment plan.
- Act as if you were feeling OK. What would you do if your emotional problems were no longer an issue? Do it now! Refuse to play the victim and you will see change.
- Own your issues. What gives you joy and causes you grief is unique to you. Sometimes we assume that others feel the same way we do when

they don't. Or we assume that others are just like our father or our mother when they are not. When you find yourself overreacting, ask yourself what you are being reminded of. When your husband criticized your meal, did it remind you of your dad never thinking you were good enough? If so, talk about it with your husband and you will find it easier to keep the past out of the present.

- Let go of false guilt. If we have confessed and turned away from some sin in our life, we should no longer have guilt. False guilt can lead to depression. Imagine yourself throwing off the burden of false guilt and walking free.
- Admit anger, but learn to control it. Denying anger is detrimental to you and your loved ones. But giving anger free reign is just as dangerous. Taking care of your own needs for rest, exercise, and recreation can decrease angry episodes. When you do get angry, evaluate the thoughts behind the anger. Are they realistic? Give yourself a time out to calm down and think clearly.

Resources

National Mental Health Association
(800) 969-8642
www.nmha.org

National Institute of Mental Health
(866) 615-6464
www.nimh.nih.gov

National Alliance for the Mentally Ill
(800) 950-6264
www.nami.org

Depression and Bipolar Support Alliance
(800) 826-3632
www.dbsalliance.org

Screening for Mental Health, Inc.
(781) 239-0071
www.mentalhealthscreening.org
www.stopasuicide.org

Center for Mental Health Services
www.mentalhealth.org

Twelve Step Program
www.12step.org

Children and Adults with Attention Deficit Disorder
www.chadd.org

Mental Health Outreach to Faith Communities
www.faithnet.nami.org

Notes

Introduction
1. *The Random House Dictionary,* Random House, Inc., 1973.
2. National Institute of Mental Health. *The Numbers Count: Mental Disorders in America.* NIH Publication No. 01-4584. Accessed 30 June 2001. www.nimh.nih.gov/publicat/numbers.cfm.

Chapter One
1. Brenda Ely, M.S. "Eating Disorders—Feeding the Hungry Heart." Alpha Care Therapy Services. Life Skills Seminar. Mt. Paran North Church of God, Marietta. Sept. 14, 1994.
2. Ibid.
3. Kathryn J. Zerbe. *The Body Betrayed: a Deeper Understanding of Women, Eating Disorders, and Treatment.* Carlsbad: Gurze Books, 1995.
4. Ibid.
5. Dr. Elisa Shipon-Blum. "When the Words Just Won't Come Out: Understanding Selective Mutism." Selective Mutism Anxiety Research & Treatment Center. Accessed 30 Aug. 2003. www.selectivemutism.org/.

Chapter Two
1. *Webster's Dictionary and Thesaurus,* V. Nichols, 1997.
2. Anne Marie Helmenstine, Ph.D. "Does Eating Turkey Make You Sleepy?" About.Com. Accessed 06 Mar. 2008. http://chemistry.about.com/od/holidaysseasons/a/tiredturkey.htm.

Chapter Three
1. Alan Loy McGinnis. *The Friendship Factor.* Minneapolis: Augsburg Publishing House, 1979.
2. Joyce C. Hicks. "Humoring the Sick." *Raleigh News & Observer.* 15 Oct. 1998.
3. Dr. Gael Crystal and Patrick Flanagan. "Laughter is Medicine." Accessed 06 Mar. 2008. www.thecertifiedhealthnut.com/index.php?option=com_content&task= view &id=13&Itemid=34.
4. *Merriam-Webster's Dictionary,* Springfield: Merriam-Webster, Inc., 2007.
5. Dr. Daniel M. Landers, "The Influence of Exercise on Mental Health." Accessed 02 Mar. 2008. http://www.fitness.gov/mentalhealth.htm.

Chapter Four
1. *King James Bible.* New York: Penguin Group, 1973.
2. Helen DeRosis, M.D. *Women and Anxiety: A Step-by-Step Program for Managing Anxiety and Depression.* New York: Hatherleigh Press. Revised edition, 1998.

Chapter Six
1. National Institute of Mental Health. *Generalized Anxiety Disorder.* Accessed 03 Mar. 2008. www.nimh.nih.gov/.
2. Ibid.

Chapter Eight

1. "Physical Causes of Mental Illness." National Advice Service Fact Sheet. Mental Health Shop. 20 Dec. 2007. Rethink and Mental Health Media. Accessed 02 Mar. 2008. www.rethink.org/about_mental_illness/what_causes_mental_illness/physical_causes_of_m.html.
2. Robert C. Bransfield, "Microbes and Mental Illness." Accessed 05 Mar. 2008. www.mentalhealthandillness.com/Articles/MicrobesAndMentalIllness.htm.
3. Ronald Kotulak. *Inside the Brain.* Kansas City: Andrews McNeel Publishing, 1996.
4. Henri Nouwen. *The Wounded Healer.* New York: Doubleday, 1979.
5. Edward Hallowell, M.D. and John Ratey, M.D. *Driven to Distraction: Recognizing and Coping with Attention Deficit Disorder from Childhood through Adulthood.* New York: Pantheon Books, 1994.
6. Ibid.
7. Ibid.

Chapter Nine

1. David D. Burns, M.D. *Feeling Good: The New Mood Therapy.* New York: Avon Books, 1995.

Chapter Ten

1. Bill Hendrick. "Men: It's OK to Seek Help—Male Depression Gets Much Needed Attention." *Cox News Service.* 03 May 1997. Accessed 06 Mar. 2008. http://archive.southcoasttoday.com/daily/05-97/05-03-97/b01li086.htm.
2. Terrance Real. *I Don't Want to Talk About It: Overcoming the Secret Legacy of Male Depression.* New York: Fireside, 1998.
3. Stanley Coren. *The Left-Hander Syndrome: The Causes and Consequences of Left-Handedness.* New York: Vintage Books. 1992-1993.
4. Kimberly Read and Marcia Purse. "Bipolar Disorder: Vincent Van Gogh." About.Com. Accessed 02 Mar. 2008. http://bipolar.about.com/od/celebrities/p/vangogh.htm.

Chapter Eleven

1. Dr. Jack Wheeler. "Freedom and the Zek's Ant." *Life Enhancement* May 1998: 19-21.
2. Lyric W. Winik. "Let Go of Stress." *Parade* 11 July 1999: 4-6.
3. Vladimir Bernik, M.D. "Stress: the Silent Killer." *Brain and Mind Magazine.* Aug./Nov. 1997.
4. Marilyn Geewax. "Sleep Deprivation Becoming Costly." *Atlanta Journal-Constitution* 08 Feb. 1998, sec. H: 2.
5. Nick Glozier, M.D. "Workplace Effects of the Stigmatization of Depression." *Journal of Occupational and Environmental Medicine* 40 (1998): 793-800.
6. Otto F. Wahl, Ph.D. *Telling is Risky Business: Mental Health Consumers Confront Stigma.* New Brunswick: Rutgers University Press, 1999.
7. David Hemsath and Leslie Yerkes. *301 Ways to Have Fun at Work.* San Francisco: BK Books, 1998.
8. Frank Minirth, M.D.; Paul Meier, M.D.; Don Hawkins, Th.M.; Chris Thurman, Ph.D.; and Richard Flournoy, Ph.D. *The Stress Factor: Thriving Emotionally and Spiritually in the Turbulent '90s.* Chicago: Northfield Publishing, 1992.

Chapter Twelve

1. National Institute of Mental Health. *The Numbers Count: Mental Disorders in America.*
2. "Sleep Apnea." *National Heart Lung and Blood Institute.* 08 Feb. 2008. Accessed 03 Mar. 2008. www.nhlbi.nih.gov/health/dci/Diseases/SleepApnea/SleepApnea_WhatIs.html.
3. "Post-Traumatic Stress Disorder." *National Institute of Mental Health.* 06 Mar. 2008. National Institute of Mental Health. Accessed 08 Mar. 2008. www.nimh.nih.gov/.
4. "Fibromyalgia." *Medline Plus.* 04 Feb. 2008. National Institute of Health. Accessed 08 Mar. 2008. www.nlm.nih.gov/.
5. Dr. Rodger Murphree. "Are Fibromyalgia Patients Crazy?" *Dr. Rodger Murphree's Health News.* Accessed 08 Mar. 2008. www.drmurphreestore.com/arefmspatcrazy-opt2.html?gclid=CJuA1djSgJICFQEelgodt2JJ9g.
6. Jan Silvious. *Please Don't Say You Need Me.* Grand Rapids: Zondervan, 1989.
7. Dale Short. "Light Out of Darkness: Depression and Creativity—A Link?" *UAB Magazine* Jan.-Feb. 1997: 4-7.

Chapter Thirteen

1. Benedict Carey. "Stress and the Company We Keep." *Total Well-Being* Jan.-Feb. 1998: 2-5.
2. Carol Hart. *Secrets of Serotonin.* New York: Lynn Sonberg Book Associates, 1996.

Chapter Fourteen

1. Tipper Gore. "Toward Understanding our Total Health," Discovering Ourselves: the Science of Emotion Executive Summary. Library of Congress, Washington D.C. Project on the Decade of the Brain. 06 May 1998. Accessed 08 March 2008. www.loc.gov/loc/brain/.
2. Julie Schweitzer, Ph.D. "Brain Function in Attention Deficit Hyperactivity Disorder (ADHD)." Society for Neuroscience. Brain Awareness Week. Emory University, Atlanta. 16 Mar. 1999.
3. Ibid.
4. Rick Weiss. "Chronic Anxiety Gene Reportedly Found." *Atlanta Journal-Constitution* 25 Aug. 1997, sec. A.
5. National Institute of Mental Health. *The Numbers Count: Mental Disorders in America.*
6. Michael Davis, Ph.D. "Brain Systems Involved in Fear and Anxiety." Society for Neuroscience. Brain Awareness Week. Emory University, Atlanta. 16 Mar. 1999.
7. Elsevier (2007, September 18). Women More Depressed And Men More Impulsive With Reduced Serotonin Functioning. *ScienceDaily.*
8. "Women are At Greater Risk for Depression Than Men." *National Institute of Mental Health.* 08 Mar. 2008. Accessed 09 Mar. 2008. www.nimh.nih.gov/.
9. Dr. James Dobson. "Dr. Dobson's Solid Answers." *Focus on the Family.* Sept. 1998: 5.
10. Jane O. Hansen. "A Perilous Prescription: Kids 'At the Bottom of the Barrel.'" *Atlanta Journal-Constitution* 13 June 2004, sec. A: 15.
11. Ibid.
12. Gwen Ifill and David Satcher, M.D. Interview. "Living with Mental Illness: Science Shows Mental Illness Can Be Treated." *Online NewsHour.* 07 June 1999. Accessed 08 Mar. 2008. www.pbs.org/newshour/.

Discussion Questions

1. In what section would you look for *I'm Not OK* at your local bookstore? Self-help? Humor? Memoir? Religion? Health and Wellness? Why?

2. What would you say is the prevailing theme of *I'm Not OK*? What other themes weave their way through this "semi-mental" journey?

3. What was the biggest "take-away" you "took away" from *OK*?

4. Did you have a hard time believing that every one of the author's stories or anecdotes was 100% true?

5. Can you relate to any of the author's childhood quirks and compulsions? Did you ever have the cooties?

6. In your opinion, was Shelley Hussey's family of origin dysfunctional, based upon your understanding of the word?

7. The author, as an adult, has a well-developed sense of humor, but do you think that she was "funny," i.e., "entertaining," as a child?

8. What was something you learned about mental illness that you did not know before you cracked open this book?

9. Did God ever disappoint the author? How would you describe her spiritual life?

10. How did young motherhood affect the author's relationship with her husband?

11. Why do you think the author's husband was so against her appearing on the Donahue show?

12. Why do you suppose the Hussey children don't remember their mother as being all that dysfunctional?

13. Describe how the author dealt with her cooties/bugs/mental turmoil as a a) child, b) teenager, c) young adult, d) new mom, e) mom with teenagers, and f) middle-aged empty-nester wife. Do you think she's finally gotten it all together?

14. What was the turning point in the author's struggle to get balance back in her life?

15. Were you satisfied with the ending?

The Cooties Project

If you've been touched by *I'm Not OK, You're Not OK,* then whether you like it or not, you have the cooties. The only way to get rid of the cooties is to:

- Offer this book as a gift to an OK or Not OK friend or family member.
- Write about the book on your blog. (If you don't have one, that's OK.)
- Direct readers to the author's web site: www.shelleyhussey.com.
- Write a book review for your local paper, www.amazon.com, or www.barnesandnoble.com.
- Buy several books and donate them to local churches, mental health clinics or offices, prisons, AA chapters, or other nonprofit/charitable organizations that deal with mental health issues and consumers. Volume discounts are available when purchasing six or more books.
- If you are acquainted with influential people who counsel or treat patients with anxiety and/or depression, suggest that they read and review *I'm Not OK* for their web site, newsletter, or other publication.
- Discuss *I'm Not OK* with everyone you know, whether they're OK or Not. Send out an email blast, post on a forum, text message, or call them. If they don't respond, get in the car and drop in on them. Last resort: snail mail.
- Purchase *I'm Not OK* for your book club members. (Discussion questions available on previous page or at www.shelleyhussey.com.)
- Contact the author for a speaking engagement:

    Email ~ shelley@shelleyhussey.com

    Web ~ www.shelleyhussey.com

    www.harperink.biz

    Fax ~ 770.216.1513

Made in the USA
Middletown, DE
08 April 2018